A

Leading
Insights

Mental Health & Well-Being

ACSI

STRONGER TOGETHER

Printed in the United States of America

28 27 26 25 24 23 22   1 2 3 4 5 6 7

Edited by Swaner, Lynn E.

ACSI Leading Insights: Mental Health and Well-Being

ISBN 978-1-58331-199-8

eISBN 978-1-58331-222-3

Catalog#: 6681
        e6681

Designer: Lisa Ruppert

Association of Christian Schools International
731 Chapel Hills Drive • Colorado Springs, CO 80920
Care Team: 800.367.0798 • www.acsi.org

CONTENTS

Introduction

Lynn E. Swaner, *Series Editor*

At the heart of Christian schools' missions is ministry to children. Christian educators desire that students flourish and achieve their God-given potential both educationally and spiritually. And yet, the reality of living in a fallen world means that every student will experience brokenness at some point in their lives, whether from family issues, relational conflict, trauma, poor self-image, social pressures, or a variety of other sources. And research suggests that mental health issues are on the rise among today's school age students; the American Psychiatric Association found in 2017 that 34 percent—*over one-third*—of students were being treated for some sort of mental health issue, compared to 19 percent of students in 2007 (Ketchen et al. 2018).

Most Christian school leaders and teachers perceive the urgency of this trend and desire to care for the whole student. Yet most will find themselves unprepared to meet students' needs, as addressing students' mental health concerns is not typically part of either formal educational preparation or on-the-job training for Christian educators. Complicating matters further, many Christian schools do not have the resources necessary for hiring full-time, qualified mental health personnel on staff. These realities can create a serious gap in Christian schools' duty to care for individual students in need, as well as to provide a healthy learning environment conductive to all students' flourishing.

This is to say nothing of the growing mental health concerns for educators, who face increasing levels of stress and burnout (Miller et al. 2020). These trends have only been exacerbated by the COVID-19 pandemic (Will 2021) with Christian school leaders citing overwork of teachers and the mental health of all staff as their top concerns (Swaner and Lee 2020). While troubling in and of itself, the decline in educator well-being is even more concerning because of its potential impact on students; as research has shown, "teacher burnout appears to affect the stress levels of the students they teach" (Lever et al. 2019, 6).

These concerns—and the corresponding risk to students, leaders and teachers, and the school community as a whole—can be mitigated if schools become more proactive and intentional in addressing student and educator mental health. This will certainly require increases and improvements in schoolwide prevention efforts, safety nets, systems of care, collaborative support teams, staff training, and clear policies and procedures. But it will also mean developing a whole-school approach to well-being—one that is grounded in a biblical philosophy of education and tailored to each school's unique context. Research has demonstrated that constructs within the Flourishing Schools domain of well-being are correlated with flourishing in the Christian school setting (Swaner and Wolfe 2021), including stress (feelings of being overwhelmed for teachers and leaders) and resilience (students' ability to handle stress effectively and respond well to difficult situations).

This issue of ACSI's *Leading Insights* series aims to help Christian schools to develop systematic programs and policies to not only address mental health concerns of students, but also promote overall student well-being. This unique resource draws upon research and best practices in the field of school-based mental health, with the goal of helping Christian educators—whatever their school setting, population, and resources—to care well for individuals and the entire school community. To this end, the monograph is divided into three sections:

- In the first section, on *Philosophy and Research*, chapters address topics like defining well-being and developing a schoolwide philosophy of mental health (Chapter 1); understanding factors, influences, and trends impacting student mental health (Chapter 2); and exploring unique factors affecting faith-based schools (Chapter 3).

- In the second section, on *Christian School Perspectives* of mental health and well-being, readers will gain insights from a school counselor in a Christian school setting (Chapter 4); a director of evaluation services who specializes in supporting students in the classroom through trauma-informed instruction (Chapter 5); and two wellness advocates and consultants who explore educator well-being and the importance of leader and teacher mental health (Chapter 6).

- In the final part of the monograph, on *Programs and Practices*, licensed professional counselors share specifics around how schools can develop a comprehensive approach to student mental health and well-being, including core components for care (Chapter 7), how to systematize support for students (Chapter 8), and the basics of crisis intervention in the school setting (Chapter 9). Real-life case studies and reflection questions are also provided across several of the chapters, as well as a final resources section.

Christian educators will find this resource useful, whether their schools are just beginning the process of addressing student mental health, or have already begun developing programs and policies. When taken together, practical recommendations in these areas can help administrators to reduce their sense of vulnerability in the face of mental health concerns, while equipping all educators to care holistically for students and the school community's needs. However, while this monograph aims to be comprehensive, it should not be taken as exclusive. Throughout many of the chapters, readers will be reminded that addressing mental health and well-being in their unique setting begins with developing a partnership between the school and mental health professionals and resources in their communities. Not only are these individuals and resources key to caring for students well, but they also should be consulted as schools develop their policies, procedures, and practices in this area.

Ultimately, as we consider the mental health and well-being of our students and all within our school community, we can take encouragement from Psalm 115:14 (NIV): "May the LORD cause you to flourish, both you and your children." This blessing certainly applies to us as educators, and also to the children within our own families, but also may be extended to Christian schools as they seek to partner with parents in fulfilling their Deuteronomy 6 responsibility to disciple their children. May we seek to excel all the more at intentionally addressing student and educator mental health, with the goal of increased flourishing for all those in our care.

Part 1:
Philosophy and Research

Defining Well-Being in Christian Schools

Charlotte Marshall Powell, *Barna Group*

Lynn E. Swaner, *ACSI*

The Bible is filled with references to God's faithfulness, demonstrated in His awareness and care for the well-being of His children. In fact, we see instances in both the Old and New Testament (Gen. 28:15, Ex. 14:13, Ps. 55:22, 1 Tim. 5:8, 1 John 5:14-15) that describe the Lord's providential protection. Importantly, we see that this care is evident in the midst of the human brokenness that is ever present in our daily lives. Whether we are young adults, children, or elders, we see throughout Scripture that how we, God's children, experience life does not go unnoticed.

Well-being is a dynamic concept that includes psychological, social, and spiritual dimensions. Often, the terms well-being or wellness are used interchangeably to denote the presence of positives and the absence of negatives—for example, a person is defined as being physically well in the absence of physical ailment or sickness. The same logic is often applied to psychological well-being; thus, the presence of mental health means the absence of mental illness. This framework demands that mental health and mental illness exist on a continuum as polar extremes. Many professionals and researchers in the field of mental health question this continuum and ask whether better terminology—such as human flourishing (Keyes 2007)—could be used to promote a more positive view of mental well-being.

But is that how the Bible defines well-being? Informed by Scripture, well-being reflects a comprehensive (physical, cognitive, affective,

> Informed by Scripture, well-being reflects a comprehensive (physical, cognitive, affective, behavioral) view and approach that acknowledges the complexity of human beings who are fearfully and wonderfully made (Psalm 139:14).

behavioral) view and approach that acknowledges the complexity of human beings who are fearfully and wonderfully made (Ps. 139:14). A biblical view of well-being also acknowledges the factors of here-and-now environmental influences—such as peer groups, family dynamics, and life stressors—as well as the eternal purpose of humanity and our dependence on God, in whom we live and move and have our being (Acts 17:28). We believe that such a view honors our biblical responsibility to rely on God through prayer and other spiritual disciplines, appreciates that human beings are complex though fallen creations, and recognizes that God has graciously gifted us with knowledge and tools that can be used to effect healing and restoration in this fallen world. While well-being can be complex and at times complicated, "the gospel impacts every area of our lives and God can—and does at times—supernaturally heal every kind of illness. Yet, God often chooses to do so through an approach that includes prayer, study, Christian community, and medical intervention" (Stetzer 2013).

Well-Being in Childhood and Adolescence

It may be surprising to learn that when viewed in light of human history, our understanding of childhood and adolescence as distinct developmental stages is relatively new. Until the late nineteenth century, children's experiences (including child labor and teen marriage, which are still common in many parts of the world) looked remarkably similar to that of adults. This changed in most Western countries when economic shifts brought a need for a skilled labor force (best developed through formal education), which resulted in the establishment of compulsory public education, child labor laws, and scientific investigation of child and adolescent development in the early twentieth century (Meece 2002).

Many argue that the children and teenagers of today are influenced by societal shifts not unlike those brought on by the industrial revolution a century and a half ago. But whereas the printing press, sewing machine, and automobile revolutionized life for earlier generations, current generations of students experience a technological revolution on almost a yearly basis (or with the newest version of the iPhone, whichever comes first). Andy Crouch (2017) writes in *The Tech-Wise Family*, "Technology is literally everywhere... not only the devices in our pockets but the invisible electromagnetic waves that flood our homes. This change has come about overnight, in the blink of an eye in terms of human history and culture" (16). The impact of the technological revolution is not always a positive one; as Miller, Latham, and Cahill (2017) assert, for many children and adolescents "the 'Gutenberg to Google' revolution has generated a perfect storm of discontent, dysfunction, and disengagement" (4) in school. And of course, technological change is but one of many significant shifts occurring today (including changes in social values and conceptions of morality, disintegration of the traditional family, and marginalization of faith and religion).

Certainly, readers—having been through childhood and adolescence themselves—can recall the physical, emotional, intellectual, and social challenges that occur during the school years. However, the rapid period of change occurring today makes most students' experience of growing up not only vastly different from those of their teachers, but also more marked by mental health issues. For example, some researchers suggest that anxiety, in particular, is becoming a normative part of growing up. As reported in *The New York Times* (Williams 2017):

> The fidget spinner is nothing but nervous energy rendered in plastic and steel, a perfect metaphor for the overscheduled, overstimulated children of today as they search for a way to unplug between jujitsu lessons, clarinet practice and Advanced Placement tutoring. According to data from the National Institute

of Mental Health, some 38 percent of girls ages 13 through 17, and 26 percent of boys, have an anxiety disorder.

In addition to anxiety disorders, self-injurious behavior like cutting is on the rise (Peterson 2008), and data presented at the 2017 Pediatric Academic Societies Meeting pointed to a doubling of hospital admissions for thoughts of suicide or self-harm in young children and adolescents over the past decade (Fottrell 2017). Another study reported a 24 percent increase in inpatient hospitalization of children for mental health and substance abuse over a three-year period (CDC 2013). All these trends have only been heightened by the COVID-19 pandemic that impacted schools and communities worldwide (Racine et al. 2021).

Most Christian school administrators and teachers can confirm that their schools are not impervious to these trends. While engagement with faith-based organizations and resources is often a protective factor when it comes to mental illness and substance abuse (SAMHSA 2015), Christians are not immune to mental health challenges. In fact, the Bible shows that even the faithful struggle with anxiety (Prov. 12:25), fear (Josh. 1:9), depression (Ps. 42:11), and mental anguish (Ps. 6:2-3). Christian educators should expect to encounter students with these struggles, given the fallen world in which we live and the weakness of the human condition. With all indications seeming to point to a significant rise in mental health concerns among today's children and youth, amplified by the effects of the pandemic era, adequately addressing the mental health needs of students needs to be a priority for educators in Christian school settings.

As much as we might wish it, students don't set aside their mental health needs when they come through the school doors. Scripture is clear that we have a mandate to care for those who are hurting and in need, by bearing another's burdens, and so fulfilling the law of Christ (Gal. 6:2, Rom. 15:1a). With this in mind, most Christian schools' missions have at the center of them the holistic education of the mind *and* the heart. This requires that we proactively address well-being through our programs and curricula. How Christian schools, administrators, and other staff participate in forming both a culture and practice of awareness and support for mental health concerns will necessarily shape the well-being and perception of well-being for their students.

First Steps/"Do Now"

While the remainder of this monograph offers many practical strategies for addressing well-being in Christian schools, it is important to pause at the beginning to reflect on the broader picture discussed in this chapter. To this end, we recommend two valuable exercises for Christian schools:

1. *Conduct a Self-Audit.* Purposefully gauge your and your school's awareness of your students' mental health needs. Gather a cross-constituency group to ask questions about how the leadership team, teachers, and others address those needs, including:

   • Do you have a grasp of what kinds of mental health needs are present in your student body?

   • Are your efforts to meet those needs intentional, having originated in an articulated philosophy and approach? How does the biblical mandate to care for students fit into the philosophy?

   • Are efforts consistent across staff and divisions/depart-ments, or are they inconsistent or haphazard?

- Are efforts proactive, or largely reactive?

- Is your school's approach to addressing mental health needs in keeping with the laws and requirements of your state? In addition to your legal obligations, what are the requirements of the school's insurance carrier? Who can you ask to help you in answering these questions (i.e. school attorney, public school counterparts, state office for nonpublic schools)?

2. *Put It in Writing.* Your school may have policies and procedures written down for addressing mental health concerns. However, at the outset, does your school have an articulated *philosophy* for how you approach these needs in general? If not, consider:

   - Creating a committee comprised of school leadership, select teachers, the school nurse, any counseling and resource staff, parents, and area mental health professionals in your networks. If yours is a church-sponsored school, include representation from the pastoral staff.

   - Tasking the group with researching and then writing out your school's philosophy and overall approach to mental health.

   - Having the group look at the results of the self-audit and identify gaps. Consider ways to fill those gaps in practice.

   - Examining any existing policies and procedures, and where they do not align with your school's overall philosophy, work to align them.

This foundational work may seem nonessential for school leaders who are pressed for answers as to how to deal with students' immediate mental health needs or crises. However, ultimately it will help positively position your school and staff for handling those needs with intentionality, consistency, and integrity—with a focus on the school's Christ-centered mission, achieved through a holistic education that is grounded in biblical truth and focused on flourishing.

Understanding Student Mental Health: Trends, Influences, and Practices

Adam Wilson, *Denver Seminary*[1]

Over the past several decades, researchers have noted a marked increase in symptoms of mental illness among the U.S. population, particularly among youth (Whitney and Peterson 2019). Approximately 10 percent of American children between the ages of 3-17 currently struggle with a diagnosed emotional disorder (HRSA 2021). Alongside the emotional and relational impacts of escalating mental health struggles (e.g., suicide, disrupted family systems), it has become increasingly clear that there are also considerable economic costs to disregarding mental health issues as well as significant financial benefits to prevention and intervention programming (McDaid, Park, and Wahlbeck 2019; Knapp and Wong 2020).

Understanding and implementing evidence-based practices surrounding student mental health can prevent or mitigate these issues. This chapter seeks to provide an abbreviated literature review of influencing factors surrounding student mental health and staff preparedness to meet these needs.[2] This broad map of the landscape of published research can help inform Christian school leaders' efforts to best support the wellness of their communities.

Mental Health Trends Among Youth

While an apparent decline in mental health cuts across all age and demographic categories, youth have displayed particularly concerning

---

[1] With additional contributors Kelsey Hauser, Elizabeth Meier Thornton, Brittany Miller, Laura Miller, and Brooke Volpone.

[2] It should be noted that much of the research on mental health and well-being has been conducted from a secular perspective. As there has been little research on faith-based school communities, Chapter 3 shares findings of a qualitative case study in one Christian school and highlights specific themes that emerged in that setting.

increases in symptoms such as depression, suicidality, and anxiety (CDC 2020). Understanding these trends, which naturally impact schools, is important for educators in all school sectors.

Depression and Suicidality

Between 2009 and 2019, U.S. youth reported a significant increase in feelings of loneliness, sadness, and suicidal thoughts. Even more concerning, there has been a corresponding increase in suicide attempts and completed suicides (Ivey-Stephenson et al. 2020). It is crucial to note that this increase is not a minor or temporary spike. In fact, between 2007 and 2018, suicide rates among adolescents increased 57.4 percent, making suicide the second most common cause of death among 12- to 19-year-olds in the U.S. (Curtin 2020). It appears these trends have only been exacerbated by the COVID-19 pandemic, with an overall increase in reported symptoms of anxiety and depression among adults (Jia et al. 2021) and youth (Racine et al. 2021).

While an apparent decline in mental health cuts across all age and demographic categories, youth have displayed particularly concerning increases in symptoms such as depression, suicidality, and anxiety.

Anxiety

Alongside depression and suicidality, there has been a corresponding increase in anxiety among youth across the globe, particularly during the COVID-19 pandemic (Racine et al. 2021). Anxiety stems from an overactive threat response in the brain and body, leading to physiological (e.g. rapid breathing, increased heart rate) and cognitive symptoms (e.g., decreased logic, decreased processing speed), ultimately reducing success in activities such as test-taking and sports performance (Getz 2014). Thus, a child's anxiety as well as pressure to perform inevitably decrease performance, likely leading to further increased anxiety. These pressures may be a student's perception and may not truly come from another person (e.g., teacher, parent) or system (e.g., college entrance requirements, sports recruiters). Yet, many educators, parents, and students report that they have experienced and observed a gradual escalation in the intensity of expectations surrounding both academic and sports performance for youth (Meier Thornton et al. 2021).

Trauma

One in three children in the U.S. population has experienced at least one adverse childhood experience, or ACE (HRSA 2021). ACEs are defined as events (e.g., divorce, parent death, mistreatment) in a child's life that create a higher risk for long-term negative consequences such as decreased mental health and wellness (HRSA 2021). Exposure to ACEs is linked to lower school attendance and a decrease in both short- and long-term academic performance (Hinojosa et al. 2019; Kiesel, Piescher, and Edleson 2016). Experiencing trauma can lead to a decrease in children's cognitive and emotional regulation skills, which impacts the classroom (Sciaraffa, Zeanah, and Zeanah 2018) and their success in an academic setting (Greene 2009). In many schools, a predominantly punitive approach is used with many students who struggle with emotional and behavioral problems, in which discipline is used to redirect student misbehavior. It is vital that schools break this pattern of using primarily discipline-based practices with children affected by trauma and replace them with trauma-informed educational practices, which are crucial in helping students with emotional dysregulation resulting from ACEs (see Chapter 5 for discussion of trauma-informed practices in schools).

Mental Health in Schools

Perhaps not unexpectedly, as mental health symptoms increase across the U.S., the nation's school systems face a growing tide of mental health-based needs among students (Osagiede et al. 2018). Unfortunately, many school systems have struggled to adequately meet these needs, resulting in a call for increased school-based mental health services, such as social-emotional learning (SEL) curricula, and school-based mental health staff like school counselors (Herman et al. 2021). Even educators and school staff with some degree of mental health training desire increased training and resources to effectively support student mental health. For example, the American School Counseling Association reports that a vast majority of school counselors express an "extreme" desire and need for professional development in the areas of mental health (87 percent) and student social-emotional skill development (86 percent) (ASCA 2021, 16).

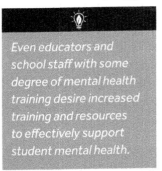

Even educators and school staff with some degree of mental health training desire increased training and resources to effectively support student mental health.

Influences on Student Mental Health

A first step in addressing these mental health trends within the school context is to understand better the various influences that contribute to the well-being of children and young people. While there are many that can be identified, there are a number of factors are well-documented in the literature and are of particular interest for educators, namely: family influence and parenting style; identity development; resilience; emotional regulation and intelligence; social media; population-specific needs; and the reciprocal relationship between educator burnout and student mental health.

Family Systems and Mental Health

Smith (2004) identifies a clear correlation between the health of an individual's parents and the mental health of a student. Increased parental anxiety (Wood et al. 2003), depression, and overall mental health issues (Black et al. 2021) in parents are correlated with similar issues in their children. Additionally, a child who has a relative with mental illness is more likely to have poor educational, social, and emotional outcomes (HRSA 2021). The stability of a child's home life and the degree to which they receive emotional and academic support at home will invariably impact their success and well-being at school. Nevertheless, Smith (2004) points out that it is imperative to acknowledge the effectiveness of many parents and family systems in supporting their children amid deep struggles. In fact, among students suffering from depression and suicidal tendencies, increased parental support is shown to reduce levels of depression and suicide attempts (LeCloux et al. 2016). The student's perception of strong familial support appears to decrease their overall sense of isolation and may even decrease their need for mental health intervention.

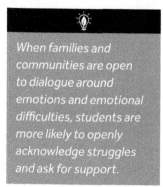

When families and communities are open to dialogue around emotions and emotional difficulties, students are more likely to openly acknowledge struggles and ask for support.

A student's willingness to seek help surrounding emotional and psychological issues is related to how they believe their family will respond to their requests for support (LeCloux et al. 2016). If they believe their family system or culture will respond negatively to their requests or needs, they are less likely to seek support (Nada-Raja, Morrison, and Skegg 2003). This fact emphasizes the potential impact of stigma around wellness and mental health. When families and communities are open to dialogue around emotions and emotional difficulties, students are more likely to openly acknowledge struggles and ask for support.

Parenting Style

Parenting style is shown to have a profound impact on the emotional and social outcomes of children, as it sets the emotional tone for the family system (Argyriou, Bakoyannis, and Tantaros 2016). For example, family systems which function from a more rigid authoritarian style tend to create an emotional context filled with criticism and emotional dysregulation. Shaw and Starr (2019) report how this type of home environment is associated with higher levels of emotional and behavioral problems for children. Likewise, a permissive or indulgent parenting style, defined by a high level of parental warmth but a low level of behavioral control, is shown to lead to higher levels of emotional and behavioral problems later in life (Cui et al. 2019). Correspondingly, parental overinvolvement, sometimes called "helicopter" or "snowplow" parenting, is associated with higher levels of entitlement (Fletcher et al. 2019), a limited ability to persevere (Schiffrin et al. 2019), and even higher rates of depression and anxiety (Cui et al. 2019).

Finally, authoritative parenting, as defined by a high level of parental empathy and warmth alongside a high level of control surrounding behavior and expectations (Pinquart and Gerke 2019), is shown to lead to lower levels of adverse behavioral and emotional outcomes, higher self-esteem in children, and increased social and emotional skills (Argyriou, Bakoyannis, and Tantaros 2016). This flexible yet firm style of parenting appears to promote a child's ability to make independent decisions, thus building their personal capabilities while still scaffolding the learning process to facilitate the development of positive emotional, social, and organizational skills (Fingerman et al. 2012; Schiffrin et al. 2014).

Identity Development

One of the central tasks of childhood, particularly adolescence, is developing a stable and healthy sense of identity (Erikson 1968). This sense of self is shaped through the interplay of a person's genetic characteristics and environmental influences (e.g., home life, peers, cultural context, etc.). While any one of these areas of influence can profoundly shape the identity of a child, the influences of peer and family systems are especially potent (Spies Shapiro and Margolin 2013; Xie et al. 2018). These influences can be both positive (Riekie, Aldridge, and Afari 2017) and damaging (Mahoney, Harris, and Eccles 2006; Verhoeven, Poorthuis, and Volman 2019). Additionally, a child's cultural background is shown to have a significant impact on overall mental well-being, and can have a positive impact if affirmed (Fisher et al. 2014).

An additional powerful influence on identity development appears to be the student's school. In a review of the literature on the impact schools and educators can have on student identity, Verhoeven, Poorthuis, and Volman (2019) found that schools often have both intentional and unintentional influences on student identity. They point to studies describing how academic or athletic achievement standards can create a framework by which children disproportionately shape their identity and worth based on real or perceived pressures. Encouragingly, intentional identity-focused learning experiences (e.g., in-depth conversations around strengths and interests), facilitated by supportive educators, can positively impact the identity and self-worth of students (Fisher et al. 2014; Verhoeven, Poorthuis, and Volman 2019).

Resilience

Resilience, an aspect of overall social and emotional health and identity, is an attribute that is developed when someone experiences challenge(s) and yet moves forward from the experience with positive emotional and cognitive well-being (Rutter 2006). This process of experiencing challenges and obtaining positive outcomes is famously described as a "growth mindset" (Dweck 2006). Others describe how resilience develops with exposure to short-term stressors that fall within a person's ability to cope (Rutter 2012). Thus, the nature by which a home or school environment facilitates the development of positive coping skills (e.g., self-control, determination) appears to directly impact the development of a student's resilience (Agnafors et al. 2017; Moffitt et al. 2011).

One central aspect of the concept of resilience is an individual's ability to tolerate the inevitable discomfort and distress that come with challenge and hardship. The ability to manage emotional and psychological discomfort has roots in both a person's biology and social environment (Agnafors et al. 2017). It is important to note that while some individuals may be born with a genetically greater tolerance for pain or discomfort, it is a skill that can be developed throughout one's lifetime (Cummings et al. 2013), especially in an environment that promotes social-emotional skills and intelligence (Ramos-Díaz et al. 2019). The promotion of this developmental skill is especially vital as tolerance for discomfort or distress (e.g., sadness, boredom, hurt, failure, etc.) has been linked to later mental health outcomes such as depression, anxiety, and addictive behaviors (Buckner, Keough, and Schmidt 2007).

Emotional Regulation and Intelligence

A person's ability to identify emotions in themselves and others is central in their ability to express and regulate their emotional responses in a healthy manner (Argyriou, Bakoyannis, and Tantaros 2016; Walton and Hibbard 2019). It can be said that emotions serve as signals from the brain to aid in decision-making (Hiser and Koenigs 2018). Therefore, it could be argued that the development of a child's ability to understand and utilize emotional information directly impacts their success in both social and academic contexts. For example, a child may identify that they feel sad or lonely at home or school and yet not know or feel comfortable expressing that emotional need to anyone directly, leading to the child feeling more isolated and dysregulated. If, however, the adults surrounding the child can educate and model a way in which the child can tell others what they are feeling in a manner that appropriately and clearly expresses their need—a skill known as functional communication—the child can receive the support and care they need leading to increased emotional regulation (Hartley 1990; Keen, Sigafoos, and Woodyatt 2001).

While, as noted above, some children may be born with a higher level of innate emotional intelligence (EI), children are profoundly shaped by the emotional regulation and modeling of adults around them (Castilho et al. 2017). Everything from general emotional regulation and social skills to academic performance has been shown to improve in environments (i.e., school systems, home) where children observe and receive education on social-emotional skills (Lemberger-Truelove et al. 2018). Especially pertinent to educators is the finding that EI is shown to increase when students are surrounded by emotionally intelligent teachers who promote social-emotional skills (e.g., empathy, compassion for self and others) within the classroom (Lemberger-Truelove et al. 2018; Walton and Hibbard 2019). Thus, the emotional health of educators is identified as an important mediating factor in the mental health and wellness of their students (Jennings and Greenberg 2009).

Social Media

The role of social media (SM) in children's mental health is currently a heavily researched and debated topic. The literature displays a wide range of conclusions regarding the possible risks and benefits of SM use among children (Odgers and Jensen 2020). Some argue that SM is designed to align with the developmental needs of adolescents, who deeply crave social engagement and validation, leading to a higher risk for problematic usage (Odgers and Jensen 2020). West, Puszczynski, and Cohn (2021) suggest that the marked increase in anxiety among youth may be, in part, due to their constant connection and engagement, particularly through SM. Of particular concern is the impact high SM use has on decreasing student engagement in prosocial activities such as extracurricular activities and direct social engagement, as the absence of this type of involvement has been linked with higher rates of depression and anxiety (Raudsepp and Kais 2019; Fardouly et al. 2018; Lin et al. 2020; Mazalin and Moore 2004; Vannucci and McCauley Ohannessian 2019). Additionally, researchers have reported increased negative social comparison, leading to decreased self-worth, among students with higher reported SM use (Fardouly et al. 2018; Lin et al. 2020;

Nesi 2020). Poor sleep (Hadijipanayis et al. 2019; Lin et al. 2020), high-risk substance use (Guinta and John 2018; Nesi 2020), and cyberbullying are all associated with SM use (Hadijipanayis et al. 2019; Nesi 2020; Odgers and Jensen 2020).

SM may have positive effects as well, however. While the risks of projecting one's identity and self for immediate feedback from a large audience are legitimate, the task of identity exploration is central to this stage of development. Therefore, if managed well, healthy identity development could be supported by SM use (Berryman, Ferguson, and Negy 2018; Hadijipanayis et al. 2019). Creativity, social engagement, and entertainment are all factors related to identity development and likewise, can all be incorporated into SM use (Berryman, Ferguson, and Negy 2018). The ability to adjust and practice aspects of their identity through their online self or avatar can allow adolescents to gradually define the aspects of self they wish to invest in (Spies Shapiro and Margolin 2013). SM use may even foster growth in areas of social connectedness and emotional support, especially for adolescents who struggle to engage in face-to-face contexts (Odgers and Jensen 2020; Raudsepp and Kais 2019; Vannucci and McCauley Ohannessian 2019).

Population-Specific Needs

The need for adequate and effective mental health support within schools is ubiquitous yet it is particularly salient for certain populations of students. For example, for schools serving students of color and those who fall into a minority status among the nation and school system, cultural competency and equity are essential for addressing student mental health through school-based programs. In addition, for many groups of students, school-based social-emotional or mental health services are the only mental health services they receive (Ali et al. 2019). This may be due to socioeconomic factors such as dependence on limited publicly funded services (e.g., Medicaid), but can also result from a hesitancy to seek out mental health support due to stigmatization within certain cultural norms in a family and/

or cultural system (Crowe et al. 2016). This type of stigma can be especially powerful among Evangelical-oriented institutions, where a mistrust of services perceived as grounded in secular philosophy may lead to resistance or minimization of the importance of receiving mental health support (Franbutt, Clark, and Speach 2011).

In addition, it is critical to note that certain populations who identify themselves differently from the surrounding culture or population are shown to be at significantly higher risk for escalated symptoms of mental illness. Youth who identify as belonging to the LGBTQ+ community are at a significantly higher risk of suicide than the general population (Aranmolate et al. 2017; Hatchel, Polanin, and Espelage 2021). An additional example of a group at elevated risk for adverse mental health outcomes are those students who are adopted, both domestic and internationally (Keyes et al. 2008). Adoption has been described as a moral value in some Christian traditions (Firmin et al. 2017; Wrobel 2012) and thus the well-being of this population may be particularly pertinent to faith-based educational institutions, which most likely enroll adopted students. In sum, as the mental health needs of the general student population increase, schools must seek to identify and understand the unique subpopulations within their communities that may carry additional pressures.

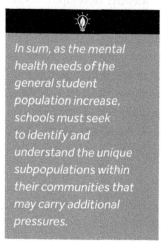

In sum, as the mental health needs of the general student population increase, schools must seek to identify and understand the unique subpopulations within their communities that may carry additional pressures.

Reciprocal Influences of Educator Burnout and Student Mental Health

As described above, student mental health is influenced by those who seek to support them, such as their teachers. Yet, it is becoming increasingly clear that educators are also deeply impacted by the needs of their students (Cook et al. 2017; Maslach, Schaufeli, and Leiter 2001). In fact, teaching is identified as having one of the highest stress outcomes of any profession (Johnson et al. 2005). Educators invest countless hours and vast quantities of mental and emotional energy in preparing and executing their responsibilities. In light of the significant increase in mental health-based needs within the school system, it is not surprising the role of the educator has become increasingly focused on student emotional and behavioral support (Reinke et al. 2011).

As educators are deeply invested in the well-being of their students, there is a tendency to quickly respond to student needs. Within school systems that contain structured policies and procedures surrounding student emotional and safety support (e.g., risk evaluations, MTSS, RTI), clear roles and responsibilities may decrease the likelihood of any one educator carrying the emotional and logistical load of supporting a student in crisis. However, far too often, school systems lack resources or clear roles/policies, leading to educator over-engagement and burnout (Chang 2009; McCarthy et al. 2010). Moreover, many over-engaged educators are, or feel, inadequate or undertrained to address student needs appropriately (Ekornes 2017; McCarthy et al. 2010).

Chang (2009) describes the emotionally taxing nature of education and how student behavior can be interconnected with levels of emotional and psychological burnout among educators. Specifically, a lack of training around student mental health support and institutional support for educators' emotional health is shown to lead to decreased overall emotional health for the educator (Ekornes 2017). This decline in educator mental health has only been exacerbated by the stresses of the COVID-19 pandemic (Baker et al. 2021). Ekornes (2017) describes how educators feel high levels of demand to competently respond to student mental health needs and yet feel a higher level of guilt and stress the more time they spend responding to those needs. Thankfully, teachers who receive mental health training report greater feelings of competency and, correspondingly, lower levels of stress. [Chapter 6 specifically addresses the topic of educator well-being.]

Evidence-Based Approaches to Promoting Student Wellness

This broad overview of mental health factors just skims the surface of the various factors involved in the wellness and mental health challenges of students today. While there may remain just as many questions as answers to the issues facing students and educators, there are several clear conclusions to assist schools and school leaders as they seek to develop wellness in their students.

Prevention

The first and foremost evidence to consider is that preventative practices are highly effective. While intervening in the crisis and struggles students face daily is an inevitable and essential aspect of school-based mental health support, just responding to the spontaneous student and family crises is ineffective (Herman et al. 2021). Instead, it is the prevention of those issues that provides the most long-term benefit to both students and schools. Wellander, Wells, and Feldman (2016) note that investing in preventive programming (e.g., SEL curriculum, suicide prevention programs, annual/bi-annual screeners for mental health and well-being, and restorative justice programs) leads not only to improved student wellness but can end up reducing the financial burdens schools carry to address student mental health struggles.

Alongside public-school educators, there is a growing call for private school educators to take a more proactive role in addressing and promoting student wellness, including the students' spiritual and mental health (Van Hoof et al. 2004; Sink, Cleveland, and Stern 2007). Regrettably, Christian schools generally have less institutional experience and financial resources supporting the development of school-based mental health resources (Van Hoof et al. 2004), apart from a more spiritual formation-focused programming (Sink, Cleveland, and Stern 2007). Moreover, Christian schools must also contend with the stigma some within their community hold regarding mental health (Franbutt, Clark, and Speach 2011).

Nonetheless, the evidence in support of school-based mental health services is robust, particularly those integrated into the school's educational culture. This makes a strong case for the necessity of educating and equipping Christian school communities to begin proactively addressing mental health. [Chapter 7 addresses the ways Christian schools can improve their capacity and ability to meet the mental health needs of their students.]

Risk Evaluation

One of the most crucial tasks of school-based mental health services is evaluating risk among the student body. Due to the alarming increases in suicidality, it is essential for schools to have policies and procedures in place to identify, evaluate, and mediate student risk. While researchers continue to collect data on the most effective programs and assessment tools, several are noteworthy (Singer, Erbacher, and Rosen 2019). Suicide prevention programs such as Sources of Strength (n.d.) and evaluation tools such as the Columbia Suicide Severity Rating Scale (Posner et al. 2008) are effectively utilized by many schools and school districts to decrease, evaluate, and address risks within the student body. [For a more in-depth exploration of the topic of risk evaluation as a part of crisis intervention, see Chapter 9.]

Multi-disciplinary Approaches

Wellander, Wells, and Feldman (2016) and Weisz et al. (2013) make a clear case for collaborative and coordinated efforts by multiple community partners (e.g., churches, schools, mental health providers, researchers) to prevent and address the mental health issues facing our youth. Through the coordinated efforts of multiple stakeholders, the myriad of factors at play in a student's life can more effectively be addressed and supported. One evidenced-based approach to facilitate this type of process is a Multi-Tiered System of Support (MTSS), which seeks to coordinate all levels of prevention and intervention within the school system (Freeman, Miller, and Newcomer 2015). Wellander, Wells, and Feldman (2016) note that the long-term benefits substantially outweigh the immediate investments needed to develop these systems. [Chapter 8 discusses how Christian schools can systemize support for students' mental health needs.]

Conclusion

As this chapter has sought to highlight, the mental health needs of students are ever growing. In parallel, the role of the educator has become increasingly intertwined with student well-being. While the needs are considerable and the severity of those needs have increased in recent decades, there is also a great deal of hope. By proactively engaging the needs of students and their families, educational communities can cultivate holistically supportive systems that seek to develop the spiritual, emotional, and mental well-being of the community. Implementing evidence-based practices such as preventative services, school-based mental health teams, policies and procedures for mental health emergencies, and engaging in a multidisciplinary approach are vital to forming a school community committed to student well-being. Through these and related efforts, effective Christian school-based student mental health and wellness support is not only possible, but attainable.

> By proactively engaging the needs of students and their families, educational communities can cultivate holistically supportive systems that seek to develop the spiritual, emotional, and mental well-being of the community.

Mental Health and Well-Being in Faith-Based Schools: A Qualitative Study

Elizabeth Meier Thornton, *Denver Seminary*
Brittany Miller, *Denver Seminary*[3]

Although there is a considerable body of research on public schools, the unique nature of faith-based schools has received less attention, particularly the mental health and wellness issues they face (Franbutt, Clark, and Speach 2011). The School Counseling Mental Health Initiative (SCMHI) at Denver Seminary is a team of researchers seeking to gain insight on overall mental health and well-being in public, private, and charter schools. Using community-based participatory research, a qualitative approach that seeks to partner with research participants, we have collaborated with a wide range of partners over the last two years to help fulfill this mission.

One partnership included a faith-based, Christian EE-12 school, from which we gleaned vital insights into the mental health needs of faith-based schools and identified integral aspects of faith-informed mental health support for students. In this chapter, we set out to share insights from this research on the unique intersection of faith, culture, and mental health in faith-based schools. While not translatable to every school setting, these insights on mental health issues, school culture, and systems to support student mental well-being are powerful and worth sharing with the Christian school sector.

Methodology

As described in Chapter 2, there are many factors that influence student mental health and well-being.[4] With these factors in mind,

---

[3] With additional contributors Kelsey Hauser, Laura Miller, Brooke Volpone, and Adam Wilson.

[4] The research described in Chapter 2 serves as the review of the literature for the present study.

we sought to obtain more information about the lived experience of students, staff, and parents in a faith-based EE-12 school by using a phenomenological partnership approach. Phenomenological research focuses on the essence of the lived experience of participants to understand a construct from the vantage point of the participants involved in the study (Flynn and Korcuska 2018). Community-based participatory research (CBPR) is a community-driven research approach that involves all stakeholders in the research process to promote co-learning and collaborative decision-making between the researchers and community members (Collins et al. 2018; Mikesell, Bromley, and Khodyakov 2013).

The study's primary research questions were: What mental health and wellness issues are faith-based schools facing? What is the lived experience of students, staff, and parents around these issues within the faith-based school environment? The study was conducted over one year in a faith-based EE-12 school in the Western United States HIPAA compliant teleconference technology was used to conduct focus groups with staff, parents, and students; using this method increased access to participants, decreased logistical and other cost factors, and increased the comfortability of participants (Gray et al. 2020). The sample size consisted of 28 administrators, educators, and staff; 13 parents; and 43 students (representing approximately 11 percent of their grade level). Participants in the study predominantly identified as white.

This unique, relational approach to community-based participatory research helped uncover themes that informed the understanding of the lived experience of individuals in a faith-based school. As a result, crucial insights surrounding mental health and wellness emerged in three broad areas: mental health concerns in the Christian school; philosophical and theological considerations; and practical challenges.

Mental Health Concerns in the Christian School

While working with our faith-based partner, we noted that mental health trends affecting children and youth[5] are present in the faith-based sector as well.

Student Mental Health

For example, in studying student mental health through the perspectives of parents, staff, and students, we learned that students were developing lower levels of resiliency and discomfort tolerance. One teacher described it this way: "The step from where the student is now, to this, to where the

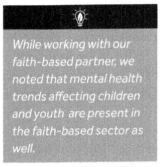

While working with our faith-based partner, we noted that mental health trends affecting children and youth are present in the faith-based sector as well.

student is in crisis... that has narrowed so much that it does not take much to push them over that line right now." One teacher noted that parents have sought to overprotect their children from all dangers by "alleviating the challenge, whatever it happens to be. Get rid of the discomfort, so the kid is happy. And so, they do not develop the ability to persevere through any kind of trial, even those things that are typical of their age."

Additionally, students today face the challenge of forming their identities within an era where everyone on social media appears to have their life together—especially for students in faith-based schools. Several described the pressure, including a middle school student who said, "Because everyone thinks because you're in a Christian school and you're a Christian—then everyone thinks like if you do one thing wrong then you're like not a good Christian, and you have to be perfect." Another high school student shared, "Social media has like a humongous impact on how we feel," and another

---

[5] As described in Chapter 2.

high school student expressed, "I feel like our school has the culture of doing everything 100 percent until you're completely burnt-out." In addition to these challenges, many students do not know how to functionally communicate or express their needs in a healthy way. One high school student captured this concept well: "I feel like our generation doesn't really know how to socialize well."

Parent and Staff Mental Health

The study also identified the theme of parent and staff mental health issues directly and indirectly impacting students' mental health. One staff member shared an observation of the parent community: "I got a strong sense of 'we're anxious.' They're anxious about their kids' success, their anxious about their futures, they're anxious about lots and lots of things, and the pressures that then come to bear on the kids are huge." Another staff member mentioned, "It gets exhausting sometimes working there... Because of everything, and it just, it just seems to never end. And you want these kids to find love and acceptance... you know through Christ." Another teacher shared, "I definitely think my mental health has been at the expense." Taken together, these adult and student mental health issues highlight the need for faith-based schools to thoughtfully conceptualize an understanding of faith-informed mental well-being and the necessity for schools to invest in systems to support holistic well-being and flourishing for everyone in the community. [See Chapter 6 for a discussion of educator well-being].

Philosophical and Theological Considerations

One important insight for the study of faith-based schools is the way in which mental health is viewed, which in turn can impact a school's mental health and wellness culture. This intersection of theology and psychology is accompanied by differences in staff, parent, and student beliefs, language, and values surrounding mental health.

Defining Mental Health

Mental health in any community, and often in faith-based communities, can be ill-defined, creating a sense of tension and anxiety on how to address the topic of mental well-being from a faith-informed perspective. A parent in our study summed it up best: "I feel, like everybody has mental health and so that's not a positive or a negative, we all work with mental health, and it's a range of sometimes being better and sometimes being more challenging." A high school student highlighted the need for a clear definition of mental health when they shared, "I guess personally what I felt is like mental health is more like, more of a chore that everyone needs to fix." The confusion around what mental health is remained a central theme throughout our interviews.

> Mental health in any community, and often in faith-based communities, can be ill-defined, creating a sense of tension and anxiety on how to address the topic of mental well-being from a faith-informed perspective.

Intertwined with faith-based school communities is the added layer of integrating their faith with their understanding of mental health. The integration process can be uniting or polarizing in a community as individuals understand faith and mental wellness from different perspectives and worldviews. For example, one teacher noted, "Prayer is such a high priority and just that the atmosphere that we have here and lifting each other up has been a huge part of, I think, what we do really well here in regard to mental health." At the same time, a middle school student saw things differently: "I'd say that another pressure is that people think that we all believe the same thing." Impacting these beliefs are the lived realities that students, parents, and staff experience.

Issues with Stigma

Perhaps not unrelated to the need to define mental health, at the partner school we found stigmas attached to mental health within the community. A high school student shared openly about this stigma, "It's not OK to be mentally ill." One teacher noted, "I think the culture around mental health at our school is confused. It's definitely not normalized, but it's also not defined." An educator, referring to the parent community, shared, "But there still is a... there's resistance. So, I think there's certain categories of mental health issues within our culture that are going to remain tamped down, unaddressed or unexpressed because ... they are related to moral issues." These stigmas were not unusual compared to other types of schools but highlighted a need for our partner school to normalize mental well-being as a part of healthy human flourishing.

Theology of Ministry

Both of these considerations—the need to define mental health and to address the presence of stigma—reflect the finding that most schools lack a defined theology of ministry (Crouch 2008). Broadly, a theology of ministry could be defined as a philosophy or ideology that informs the way in which a system or individual defines what their role is in ministry and how they view God's call to engage in the care of others. This can vary based on the community's theological and psychological beliefs, views on the nature of human beings, and model of health or wellness (Johnson 2010). A school's theology of ministry can also potentially place limitations on staffing, training, and funding (Beckman, Drexler, and Eames 2012; Mills 2003; Murray 2011).

It is imperative that faith-based schools seek to define their theology of ministry and formulate action steps to address issues they may be facing in whichever context best fits their theology. Further defining a school's theology of ministry can also assist in encouraging those involved in the ministry to maintain healthy boundaries. This is important because ill-defined boundaries can lead to staff feeling overextended and depleted both physically and emotionally, which can eventually lead to burnout (Maslach, Schaufeli, and Leiter 2001).

Practical Challenges

Our study uncovered some practical challenges when it comes to the ways that faith-based schools work to meet the mental health needs within their community. These challenges were related to both personnel and to creating systems for support.

The Personnel Challenge

Our study highlighted the unique challenges of faith-based schools in regard to personnel and student mental health issues. On one level, many faith-based schools and school staff develop authentic relationships with their students and parent community

We found that some staff at the partner school were over-engaging and supporting students to a concerning level of fatigue.

that positively impact student mental health and well-being. A teacher at our partner school noted, "I mean, truly, the teachers' involvement in these kids' lives makes a massive difference, you know. They know their names. They're loved on. They're prayed for."

At the same time, and on the flip side, we found that some staff at the partner school were over-engaging and supporting students to a concerning level of fatigue. This fatigue pointed to a lack of understanding of educators' roles, boundaries around their roles that protect both staff and students, proper mental health training, and a misguided understanding of confidentiality regarding student mental health. For example, a teacher described confusion on confidentiality: "It's hard to know how much as a teacher, I need to know, or I should know. I have had students pulled out in the past for counseling, and I haven't known what is going on... I certainly want to respect their privacy, but also, is there anything I need to be aware of or that I need to know as a teacher."

Overall, our research highlighted the need for faith-based schools need to define the roles of how staff engages with student mental health. For example, a teacher shared, "I think part of it too, kind of like our mission statement, right, we're partnering with the parents for education. We're partnering with the parents for mental health as well. I mean, that's, it's a whole encompassing person that we're dealing with, not just one or two aspects of it."

Needing Systems for Support

In working with our faith-based partner, we found that systems supporting student mental well-being and flourishing were essential. Overall, SCMHI noted another issue some faith-based schools encounter is a reactive rather than proactive approach to mental health. A teacher reflected on this reactivity, "I feel like there's definitely been a sense of survival mode, like we have to you know, get through this."

Participants from our study highlighted the need for transitional support for students coming into the school for the first time, support for students transitioning between grade levels, community-wide psychoeducation on mental health, and a clear flow for communication and collaboration amongst staff, parents, and students about students' mental health needs. Along with transitional support, both faculty and parents were requesting more community-wide psychoeducation to promote mental well-being. One parent shared, "Really we need to get more psychoeducation in the class," while an administrator shared, "We have people dealing with things they're not exactly trained for." The staff in our partner school also acknowledged they needed to develop better systems to communicate and collaborate on student mental health when a teacher shared, "That's a very difficult thing to do, to get effective collaboration. And then it's even harder to keep the collaboration going with mental health professionals." While private schools have the freedom to develop their own systems, it is vital for any school to set up a system delineating how they address students' mental health and well-being. [Approaches to systematizing support within the Christian school setting is addressed in Chapter 8].

Next Steps

In studying the lived experiences of staff, parents, and students at our partner school, we uncovered the pervasive reality of mental health as part of the human condition, and a deep desire to understand mental health and well-being through God's story of redemption. These findings beg the question of "what's next?" Whatever stage a school is at, there are practical steps that can be taken to create a culture of faith-informed mental well-being. SCMHI has identified ten achievable steps that faith-based schools can take to equip staff, students, and families with how to engage in conversations and implement systems regarding faith-informed mental well-being:

1. Conduct a school audit to assess current school culture and resources on mental well-being where staff, students, parents, and key stakeholders engage in a dialogue on defining mental health to inform the school's theology of ministry on holistic mental well-being.
2. Identify external community resources for the school (including local churches, church-based counseling centers, faith-based counselors, counselors offering reduced or sliding scale options for families or post-COVID-19 relief resources).
3. Create a crisis intervention plan.
4. Train staff on suicide prevention and mental health first aid.
5. Continue to develop connections with students, parents, and staff.
6. Create systematic meeting times for focused "kid talk" at specific grade levels.
7. Develop a resource library of free articles, digital training, and other mental health resources.
8. Seek out grant-based funding to increase the opportunity for mental health providers within the school.

9. Reach out to local research institutions like SCMHI for resources and collaboration opportunities.
10. Access the school's alumni network to identify mental health resources that aided them during school and post-graduation.

Any of these steps are options for schools to address the mental well-being within their school, regardless of how these issues currently exist in the school's culture and support systems. The chapters that follow in this monograph explore many of these steps and provide road maps for schools to engage them.

In closing, the significance of this research points to the importance of understanding faith-based schools' needs in promoting faith-informed mental well-being. It also informs how faith communities can lean into the topic of mental health with an open mind of acceptance, determination, and an understanding of their theology to make vital changes to improve school support systems and culture around holistic mental well-being.

Part 2:
Christian School Perspectives

Reflections of a School Counselor

Nancy Gillespie, *Grove City Christian School*

I will never forget the date: January 14, 2005. This was the day that I was rushed to the hospital and found out that I had just barely survived a pulmonary embolism. This was a significant day in my faith journey as I knew that God was trying to get my attention. He had given me a second chance at life, and I did not want to take that for granted. I was not quite sure what was coming, but I knew that change was around the corner. It was shortly after that day that I decided to go back to school and pursue my master's degree in counselor education so that I could become a school counselor.

Prior to this decision, I had worked with adolescents in a variety of roles. I was on staff with Young Life and was a pastor's wife for many years. In fact, I am still a pastor's wife today. I knew I loved working with adolescents, and I felt very compelled to earn that degree and start a new career path. My passion had always been to work with teens. I knew how pivotal that time in life was for me and how much I relied on trusted adults to walk alongside me. I wanted to be a trusted adult in the lives of my students.

When I was almost done with my requirements and soon would have that diploma in hand from The Ohio State University, I was excited to learn that I had an interview at Grove City Christian School (GCCS) outside of Columbus, Ohio. Was it a coincidence that I had been praying for that very school the night before I was offered the interview, as I had heard of a tragic situation involving some of their students and felt compelled to pray? I don't think so. Was it coincidence that I had been a Young Life leader in the public school across the street years prior and knew the area, the community, and the culture? I don't think so. I had the interview and never looked back.

When I was first hired, GCCS did not have a school counseling program, so I was hired as an academic counselor to help students in their academic pursuits. It did not take long for any of us to realize that to help students succeed in the classroom, it was important to peel back the layers and look at what was happening in their lives outside of the classroom. According to the American School Counseling Association (ASCA), there are three primary areas to focus on in a school counseling program: academics; career development; and social emotional development (ASCA 2022). As time went on, we were able to put in motion the beginning stages of a comprehensive school counseling program. In the years since then, the program has grown and expanded, and we have learned a lot about what it can look like in the Christian school setting, where students' needs are met and they are growing into all that God has for them. In this chapter, I hope to share a few reflections on this journey and the learning along the way.

It Takes a School

Perhaps the thing I have learned to value the most in my role as a school counselor is the importance of collaboration and relationship building. Having a supportive administration and a cooperative staff is imperative to a healthy school counseling program. It is when we work together that we can best meet the needs of students in the classroom, on the athletic field, in the halls and as they navigate their way through life. In Scripture, 1 Corinthians 12:18-20 offers an excellent illustration to point out the importance of the many different parts that need to work together to maximize the efforts of the body: "But in fact, God has placed the parts in the body, every one of them, just as he wanted them to be. If they were all one part, where would the body be? As it is, there are many parts, but one body." In the same way, each part of the Christian school needs to work together to maximize the educational experience for students.

This body of Christ at GCCS has been so significant through the years as we have navigated many tragedies. Each person plays a special role unique to them and the relationships they have cultivated within the school community. There is not a case study or a book or a graduate course that quite prepares you for having to navigate a tragedy within a school. Throughout my thirteen years at GCCS, we have faced some difficult days. I am reminded of the student that was diagnosed with a brain tumor, only for the student to lose that battle weeks after graduation. I think of the phone call I received late one night letting me know that another student had been killed in a tragic car accident. There was another phone call that I received while driving home from school: a student had suddenly lost a parent in a tragic event and the student was unaware and still in the building. I remember turning the car around and speeding back to school just to be with the student when the authorities arrived. Another incident that comes to mind is when our school was directly struck by a tornado just a few hours after school let out. Athletes, coaches, and a handful of others were on campus when it hit. We were all grateful that there was no loss of life given the considerable damage that the building sustained. While we had to suspend operations for a couple of weeks, we all knew that it could have been much worse. Throughout my time at GCCS, I have also had to say goodbye to dear colleagues and navigate my own grief while helping students and other staff with theirs.

These tragic events are not unique to our school or community. Across the world, people are faced with challenging circumstances and difficult days. This is where we have the amazing opportunity to stand out as a school. As a Christian school, we offer a message of hope, love, goodness, restoration, and peace. During each of these tragedies, our school community grew stronger. Through prayer vigils, families joining together to serve, and people giving of their time, talents, and treasures, we witnessed God's people come together time after time.

As a school counselor, my roles and responsibilities during those events were significant. They were many sleepless nights thinking about all that needed to get done. But together, we were able to offer counseling services and resources for students, staff, and families. Together we created times and locations for staff and students to gather and simply be with one another. Together, we helped students to find hope and peace while walking through intense grief. In those times, it was not about the specific role of each person but rather how we worked together collectively. Sure, we had done professional development

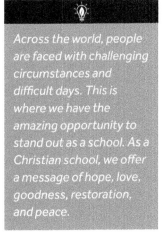

Across the world, people are faced with challenging circumstances and difficult days. This is where we have the amazing opportunity to stand out as a school. As a Christian school, we offer a message of hope, love, goodness, restoration, and peace.

about how to handle some of those things, but no amount of training can prepare a school community for tragedy and loss. The mental health and well-being of everyone was affected during those times. It was in those tragic moments that I knew my role was important. Not that there was anything special about me specifically, but rather that we had a trained professional in the building who could help staff, students, and families to navigate the difficult times. Equally important was providing resources for those in need. Partnering with local doctors, hospitals, counseling agencies, church staff, and other school counselors became a necessary commodity time and time again.

Mental Health Trends

There is a quote by George Barna that sits on the wall behind my desk: *"If you want to have a lasting influence upon the world, you must invest in people's lives; and if you want to maximize that investment, then you must invest in those people while they are young."* Now more than ever, I see the importance of that quote. Our young people are being influenced in so many ways. There are a lot of things vying for their attention and pulling on their heartstrings. There are so many

There is a quote by George Barna that sits on the wall behind my desk: "If you want to have a lasting influence upon the world, you must invest in people's lives; and if you want to maximize that investment, then you must invest in those people while they are young."

mixed messages and so much "fake news" for them to decipher. There is political unrest, racial tension, and a spirit of division in our world. Social media is the robber of time and often influences the thinking, attitudes, and behavior of students. What does that have to do with my role as a school counselor? Everything.

In the latter half of my career, I started to notice several shifts in my students. Apathy grew stronger, behaviors of some grew worse, depression and anxiety increased tremendously, and suicidal ideation became a pervasive thought in the lives of several students. Why? I began to ask more questions to try and figure out if what I was seeing was commonplace in other schools. Unfortunately, the answer was yes: These trends are very commonplace in teen culture. I collaborated with our local children's hospital as they have a top-notch behavioral health center. Together, we spoke to counselors across the state about suicide awareness and prevention and how to bring programming to schools to walk alongside students in their darkest days and provide help, resources, and partnerships with families.

As a school, we now do an annual Suicide Prevention and Awareness program called the Signs of Suicide. Each year, students are learning what do to if another student shares suicidal thoughts with them. We teach students that if they see something (in person or online), they need to say something to a trusted adult. The program also reinforces the acronym ACT (Acknowledge, Care, Tell) and encourages students to talk to a trusted adult if they are hurting and are not in a good place mentally and emotionally. This program has opened the doors to have significant conversations with students and their families. We have been able to connect many families with outside counseling agencies that offer them individual and family support. While this is a difficult week of every school year, it is also a very powerful time. For many students, it is a time to finally trust someone with what they have been going through. And some students realize from the program questionnaire that they are anxious or sad, and that it may be time to get some help.

We also began to observe that many of these issues were taking root with our younger students. Having a supportive administration and a head of school who understands the importance of school counselors in the building, we hired a counselor to serve our K-8 students and families. Our local public district does not have elementary counselors due to budget constraints; as I have talked to my counterparts in the local public school, they are keenly aware that we have an elementary counselor and wish they could, too. The needs of our youngest students are many, and in developing our program, we realized the importance of having that support person in the building. This was one of the greatest decisions we could have made, because we are supporting our younger students as these trends start to emerge, and hopefully help them to develop healthy ways of thinking, feeling, and acting, before they even arrive at adolescence with all its challenges.

The Impact of Technology

In my observations of local and national statistics and informal research, I also began to see another trend. The more students were on their phones, the more distant students seemed to be and the less likely they were to pay attention in class. American teens are in front of a screen more than seven hours a day, not including their schoolwork (Rogers 2019). As a school, we decided to do a school-wide experiment.

In February and March of 2020, just before the onset of the COVID-19 pandemic, I decided to look at what the effects were, if any, among our students from their cell phone use. I worked with our statistics class and had them help me with data collection. What we found was astonishing. Normally, our middle school students are not permitted to have their phones during the day and our high students have limited phone use. Without notifying students ahead of time, we decided to allow students to have their phones with them for one day and their notification settings had to be on. On that particular day, everyone had a piece of paper that allowed them to track their notifications through out the day. With a population of about 315 students, there were over 16,600 notifications in just one day. That averages to about 53 notifications in one school day per student. We were able to take that data and quickly turn it to a life lesson of how much our phones are a distraction.

To look at even further evidence, the next day (without letting the students know), they were not permitted to use their phones at all during the day. They even had to go "old school" and go to the office if they needed to call home. We did not collect quantitative data, but instead we had an exit questionnaire at the end of the day to see what the reaction was by students to the lack of access to their phone for the day. We were amazed at what we heard and observed from students. While some students were honest in their opinion of the experiment and they disliked being away from their phones, most students commented on how much they appreciated it. Some realized they are dealing with social awkwardness and have used their phone to avoid social interactions. Others were reunited with friends they hadn't spoken to in a while through lunchtime conversations. And many just said it was refreshing to not have the pressure of their phone and all the notifications that distracted them.

This silly little experiment reminded me of how much these young minds are being influenced by technology. It was a good reminder of how powerful the Internet, social media, and constant connection can be. While there is great value in modern technology, there are also things that we must be intentional about teaching our teens. Do they know what to do when being solicited for inappropriate pictures by a friend, let alone a stranger? Do they know what things are appropriate to post and what offers too much personal information? Are students engaging in online behavior (gaming, chatting, etc.) with complete strangers? Do they know how to block their location? Do parents know the latest apps that teens are using to mask their identity,

By having a comprehensive school counseling program in the building, we can provide information for our stakeholders and address difficult conversations around technology and culture.

whereabouts, etc.? Do parents have an understanding of teen lingo that is being used on the latest apps?

By having a comprehensive school counseling program in the building, we can provide information for our stakeholders and address difficult conversations around technology and culture. As a school we began to put articles in our parent newsletter to offer family resources around the issues of mental health, screen time, the effects of social media, and ways to set limits. We conducted professional development for our staff on the lingo and trends of apps and texting. We even hosted a parent night in conjunction with local authorities to talk to parents about digital footprints and the importance of understanding what is going on in the cyberworld. While these topics are fluid and technology is ever changing, we are doing what we can to stay in touch with cultural trends, and having a comprehensive school counseling program helps tremendously in this effort.

Then Came Along COVID-19

Do you remember the date I said that we were doing our upper school phone experiment? It was the end of February and the beginning of March of 2020. After the experiment, the goal was to encourage families to engage in conversation with their student about cell usage and screen time and to make a concerted effort as a school community to reduce our time on screens. But then, the COVID-19 pandemic came along. To this day, my students remind me of the irony that we had just talked about the effects of screen time and then within a couple of weeks we were gathered in the gym to let students know that we would have to go to remote learning for a couple of weeks. As the story goes for most Christian schools, we went to remote learning for the rest of the school year.

As a mental health worker, it did not take long to realize that we were trying to solve a problem with a problem. Educators across the country had to get creative with how to keep students engaged in their schoolwork. Technology companies boomed and words like Zoom, bandwidth, Google Hangouts, remote learning, and synchronous versus asynchronous learning became household terms. Prior to COVID-19 and the increase in screen time, researchers found that children ages four to 17 years old who used their phones seven or more hours per day were more than twice as likely to ever have been diagnosed with depression and or anxiety, treated by a mental health professional, or have taken medication for a psychological or behavioral issue (Twenge and Campbell 2018). So, what would the effects be of adding even more time in front of a screen to students? Unfortunately, I don't think we can begin to see the full effect of this as we are still amid the pandemic two years later. In fact, just this week, as I write, we had to the make the decision to go to remote learning as the cases have spiked in our community yet again. While we are not anticipating this will be a long-term decision, I am anticipating the mental health effects will have long-term effects on our precious young people.

As much as these past few years have been difficult, they have also given us the opportunity to see the best in people. Just last week when we made the announcement that we had to go remote, my office quickly filled up with students having concerns for what that would look like. For some it was simply that home was not their safe place—school was. For others, it was a fear of losing motivation while on remote learning and not being able to do that with graduation on the horizon. For others it was deeper, a sense of "what if we are out the rest of the year again?" My heart sank.

But one student who came in my office with tears in his eyes, also asked if he could pray for the school. He felt very compelled to pray for God's hand in all of this and for students to remember the One who gives us life and love. And so, at the end of the day, that dear student came over

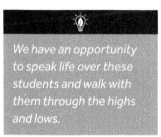

We have an opportunity to speak life over these students and walk with them through the highs and lows.

the announcements to pray for our staff and student body. It was my turn to tear up as I heard the passion in his voice for Jesus. These are the moments when we are reminded of the importance of what we do. As my principal always says, "We *get* to do this." This could not be truer. We have an opportunity to speak life over these students and walk with them through the highs and lows. Even though it can be challenging, I truly think I have the best job in the world. I love being a school counselor.

Trauma-Based Instruction:
A View from the Classroom

Betsy Winkle, *All Belong Center for Inclusive Education*

Trauma is described as "an exceptional experience in which powerful and dangerous circumstances overwhelm a person's capacity to cope" (Souers and Hall 2016, 15). Developmental trauma occurs during childhood (in utero through age 17) and can be a one-time occurrence or multiple adversities experienced over time. When children experience adversity without the support of a caring adult, that is when dysregulation—or poor management of emotional responses—occurs. As educators, we want to attend to how each child responds to traumatic events by noticing the effect on behavior.

The Adverse Childhood Experiences Study (ACES) provided a framework for understanding trauma and identified the relationship between a child's emotional experience and their subsequent mental and physical health. The trauma events noted in the study included physical, emotional and sexual abuse, physical and emotional neglect, mental illness, domestic violence, substance abuse, divorce, and incarcerated relatives (Center for Disease Control 2021). The study revealed that childhood trauma is more common than we thought. Children are especially sensitive to adversity because the brain depends on positive experiences to grow. When a child experiences significant and ongoing trauma without protective factors, the brain wires differently to adapt and prepare for an environment that is less consistent, less predictable, and less safe (Perry and Szalavitz 2017).

The COVID-19 pandemic has become a communal traumatic event for many, although not all children will experience the pandemic as a significant stressor. Traumatic events are more distressing when we do not know when they will end, the events feel out of our control, and they keep us from people that help us regulate stress (Grant 2020). We will likely not know who all is impacted and to what extent for some time, but early data indicates that there is an increase in childhood mental health challenges as evidenced by the increase in mental health emergencies (Leeb et al 2020). This means that to some extent—and often to a great extent—every classroom teacher needs to shift their instruction and classroom practices to ones that are "trauma-based," or that are grounded in an understanding of the effects of trauma.

How Trauma Impacts Student Learning and Behavior

It is critical to interpret behavior as communication. When a student with developmental trauma responds with uncharacteristic emotion or behavior to the demands of school or interactions with others, their behaviors tell us something about how they are feeling, taking in the environment, and pro-cessing their circumstances. When each of us experiences stress, our stress-response system is triggered, moving us into our fight-flight-freeze modes of responding. Hormones are activat-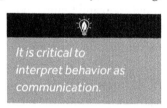ed that move our brains and bodies from thinking into responding, which helps us survive a threatening situation.

Students with a history of trauma show an increased sensitiv-ity to triggering a stress response (Burke Harris 2018). When the stress-response system is activated repeatedly, this becomes a child's natural way of processing and responding to experiences and creates dysregulation in brain functioning. A child then reacts to experiences out of the responsive and emotional areas of the brain—the *doing* brain, rather than viewing experience through the *thinking* part of the brain, which integrates emotions and experiences through rea-soning (Siegel and Payne Bryson 2012). A child's brain is particularly vulnerable because it is still developing and adapts to the stressful environment with the repetitive activation of the stress response system (Forbes 2012). Children who have experienced trauma then present with a range of behaviors: from dissociated, to disengaged, to aggressive, to over-responsive.

All of these behaviors impact learning. However, with an increased understanding of how stressful experiences impact a child's ability to stay regulated for learning and engagement, we are better equipped to support student growth and development. We can provide a supportive and caring environment focused on fostering positive relationships, and we can build each child's social and emotional skills to better manage stress.

Prioritize Relationships

Healing happens through relationships. We are hardwired for connection and trauma most often happens in the context of disrupted or unsafe relationships. In the school and classroom, prioritize building healthy and safe relationships to rebuild what was lost. Research tells us that relationships can serve as a buffer, or protective factor, to the stressors that a child is experiencing, effectively off-setting the impact of stress (Feifer 2019). For some students, teachers are a lifeline of support to stay regulated and engage effectively in learning and relationships.

An open, calm, and reflective posture toward students enhances well-being and provides space for students to stay regulated in order to learn. As educators, take the posture of an emotional scientist, not emotional judge (Brackett 2019). Be curious about the emotions your students express and the behaviors that follow. This allows us to connect with students and express empathy. Make time for relationship-building during the school day, incorporating activities to foster relationships between students and between teachers and students.

When a student's stress response is activated, there are several things adults can do. To help students work through their dysregulated state, let the big emotions come so that they will pass. Our nonverbal communication—tone of voice, body posture, calm breathing, and facial communication—will ground the student to the present moment and settle their system. Every time we remain present, calm, and reassuring, we are helping that student to learn how to calm their overactive system. With repetition, the student is better able to encounter a stressor without activating the stress-response system, allowing access to the *thinking* brain and regulated, thoughtful response.

Proactively building positive relationships can enhance classroom community to facilitate learning and decrease the need for behavior management. Two questions to consider are:

1. How do you intentionally build classroom community?
2. How do you model the importance of being known to each child in your school or classroom?

Create Safe and Supportive Environments

Consistency and predictability create safety and stability. Take the opportunity to greet students at the door as they enter the school and classroom. This creates welcome, fosters relationships, and provides a quick check of the students' affect. As administrators and teachers, be consistent in your responses to students, in your feedback and expectations, in your affect, and in your response to stress. When possible, be consistent in routines and scheduling; communicate when changes occur.

Think about the physical space students are entering, both in your school buildings and classrooms. Pay attention to the sensory input (noises, brightness, colors, smells). Sensory input can foster or hinder learning for students with heightened alertness due to stress; if students are stressed, they are less able to be engaged in learning. Provide designated space or spaces with activities and materials that can foster calm (coloring pages, headphones, manipulatives, movement) when needed. Calm-down spaces promote self-awareness and self-regulation, and guide the student back to a state of learning.

Throughout the day, embed patterned, repetitive, and rhythmic movement, music, or other sensory activities that promote self-regulation (Sorrels 2019). Use hands-on experiential activities to provide active engagement in the world. Simple science experiments can help children learn cause and effect, which is often difficult for students with developmental trauma. Provide opportunities for creative play—theater, art, and music. Imaginative and creative play provides children the opportunity to engage with their classmates, engage in a range of emotions, and practice prosocial skills within a structured and safe setting.

As you walk into your school and classroom and think about your typical school day, questions to consider include:

1. What do you feel? Does your space foster a sense of calm, safety, and predictability?
2. What are ways you can imbed stress-reducing movement or activities? Does your day include opportunities for creative play or engagement?

Build Social Emotional Skills

A school-wide approach to teaching social and emotional learning (SEL) skills fosters common language throughout the school building, providing consistent and developmentally appropriate instruction of skills including self-awareness, self-regulation, and relationship skills. Teaching SEL skills can also be embedded during the day through the questions you ask about a child's experiences, the modeling of appropriate social and emotional skills, and explicit teaching of SEL skills within your curriculum. Dr. Ross Greene (2016) identified the concept of lagging skills; if a child is struggling with something, they do not have the skills yet to appropriately deal with the situation. Identify what skills may be missing or lagging, then teach, model, practice, and reinforce the skill. Model expected behaviors, provide opportunities for students to practice or role-play what you have modeled, and use a cooperative approach to learning (Feifer 2019).

In the school setting, support student growth in building healthy coping strategies. Work with students to identify threat/stress by talking about the size of the problem in tangible terms or with visuals. Label the expected response for each type of problem. Model and teach decision-making using everyday life circumstances throughout the day or through literature. Acknowledge that stress and negative emotions will come and model a calm response to changes; this communicates to students that you will figure it out together. Develop positive affirmations and claim

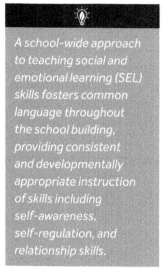

A school-wide approach to teaching social and emotional learning (SEL) skills fosters common language throughout the school building, providing consistent and developmentally appropriate instruction of skills including self-awareness, self-regulation, and relationship skills.

Scripture together to acknowledge God's ongoing presence and work in our lives, such as Joshua 1:9, "Be strong and courageous. Do not be afraid; do not be discouraged, for the LORD your God will be with you wherever you go," and Psalm 46:1, "God is our refuge and strength, an ever-present help in trouble."

Build students' emotion awareness, both in themselves and recognizing the emotions of others. Use a range of emotion words in your classroom and provide visual emotion charts to expand students' emotion vocabulary. Wonder about emotions with students, either in real-life events or through literature. Avoid labeling emotions but wonder together about what behaviors you are observing and what emotions may be underneath those behaviors. For example, if you notice a student crying, respond by saying, "You have tears in your eyes—I wonder if you are feeling sad?"

Create opportunities for children to serve to give them a greater sense of purpose and meaning. The experiences of trauma often leave a child wondering about themselves and their place in the world. Service opportunities allow students with developmental trauma to think outside of their own circumstances and see themselves as active agents of restoration. A healing-centered approach helps shift from the question of what harm happened to cause trauma, to the strengths students bring to the community and how they can be active in their own healing (Ginwright 2018). Think about how to leverage student strengths through class jobs, cross-grade tutoring or support, or community-focused group projects.

As you reflect on ways to build social emotional skills with your students, consider the following questions:

1. What social and emotional skills do you notice are lagging or missing?
2. In what ways can you begin to prioritize and embed the teaching, modeling, and practice of self-regulation, healthy coping strategies, and emotion awareness?

From Discipline to Restorative Practices

Restorative practices provide a structure for schools to prioritize relationships, proactively building the connections among staff and students that are needed to restore relationships when harm occurs. Traditional discipline practices that focus on cognitive strategies to correct behavior are likely to be less effective for students with trauma histories. Children with developmental trauma are more often operating in the reactive, emotional parts of the brain rather than the cognitive, reasoning parts of their brain. This results in decreased access to the active reasoning needed for cognitive behavior management strategies to be effective. Restorative practices keep relationships as the priority, inviting students to develop the strong and meaningful connections essential for healing from developmental trauma. When conflict occurs in the context of a strong community, the structure and consistency of the restorative process engages the voices of those involved to repair harm and restore relationships.

Restorative practices invite us to prioritize relationship building through our everyday interactions with students, embedding affective language to build emotional awareness and the connection between our emotions and behaviors. The formal structure of circles intentionally builds connections and fosters community as educators and students get to know one another. When relationships are formed, we can address conflict in a restorative way, using restorative questions. Both the person doing the harm and the student who was harmed are invited to respond to tell the story of what happened, what they have been thinking about, and what needs to happen to make it right. Those that are involved in the conflict are active participants and given agency in solving the problem (Costello, Wachtel, and Wachtel 2019). Using the tools of restorative practices, relationships are kept at the center, space is made for empathetic listening and understanding, and students are engaged in collaborative problem-solving. These help to promote healing for students who have experienced trauma.

As you examine how your classroom and school policies and procedures respond when conflict occurs, consider these questions:

1. Do your current policies and procedures rely on cognitive strategies for behavior change, or do your current practices focus on building relationships?
2. Do your current practices promote the SEL skills you are trying to develop in your students?

Supporting Staff

Not only do students need safe and supportive learning environments, but teachers do as well. It is crucial to heed and attend to symptoms of fatigue and stress in our own lives, both for our own well-being and the well-being of our students. Children who have experienced trauma can be unpredictable and require our self-regulation, emotion management, and use of positive coping skills.

To build your capacity as an educator to support hurting students, embed activities to help stay calm and regulated into your day. Allow time for connection among staff to listen, debrief, and pray together. Plan for when you are not able to be the calm, soothing presence that a child needs in the moment. Name the losses, frustrations, and challenges. Lament. Celebrate successes. Practice gratitude. Prioritize building these routines into the school day, starting each day with staff devotions, or providing a short check-out circle at the end of the day or week. And be aware of your capacity and the mental health support available in your school and community. [See Chapter 6 for discussion of well-being strategies for educators.]

As you think about your own well-being as an education, it is important to consider your thoughts and emotions throughout the school day. Ask yourself these questions:

1. At what points in your day are you most likely to lose your calm?
2. How does this manifest in your interactions with students?
3. How can you plan to respond to the stressors that will inevitably come?

Trauma-Informed Schools

The foundation of trauma-informed practice in schools requires the understanding that for a child to learn, the child's trauma must be held in mind. At the school level, this means focusing on creating a sense of safety in the school and classroom and building trusting relationships. Managing behaviors is not enough; rather, healing comes through positive, consistent relationships that nurture a child's potential. Work to create a classroom and school that fosters calm, provides consistency, and responds to challenging behavior and emotions with empathy. Schoolwide, focus on building the emotional skills of self-regulation, emotion awareness, and healthy coping strategies, which allow students with developmental trauma to spend more time in calmer, regulated states with an increased access to learning. And lean into the support of your community—children with developmental trauma can be particularly challenging. As a staff, be sure to tend to your own needs so you can better respond to the needs of your students.

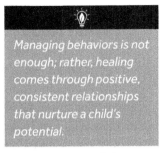

Managing behaviors is not enough; rather, healing comes through positive, consistent relationships that nurture a child's potential.

We live in a broken and fallen world, and students who have experienced trauma can remind us of the ways that we feel distant from God. Throughout the book of Psalms, David creates a picture of the range of human emotions. Psalm 13 provides the depth of that emotional range and exhibits the arc of emotions that students with developmental trauma experience: "How long, LORD? Will you forget me forever? How long will you hide your face from me?" But God invites us to be His agents of reconciliation, to restore relationship and help students see the strengths of who He has created them to be. The Psalm ends with this declaration: "But I trust in your unfailing love; my heart rejoices in your salvation. I will sing the Lord's praise, for he has been good to me." By knowing, enfolding, and walking with students with developmental trauma, we are invited to participate in God's redemptive work.

Educator Well-Being:
What About Leaders and Teachers?
Rex Miller, *MindShift*
Ginger Hill, *Good Health for Good Works*

Even prior to the COVID-19 pandemic, stress emerged in the research as a significant issue for leaders and teachers in Christian schools (Swaner, Marshall, and Tesar 2019). High levels of "battle fatigue" are common among educators, with burnout resulting from the "caregiver's dilemma"—where teachers suffer from caring too much about their students, to the point they neglect their own well-being (Miller et al. 2020). And as ACSI has shared through research on Christian schools' responses during COVID-19 (Swaner and Lee 2020), the greatest concern of Christian school leaders was overwork for teachers (77 percent), followed by the mental health of leaders, faculty, and staff (73 percent).

Our first priority in schools needs to be to take care of and restore our caregivers. Healthy, happy, and productive teachers produce engaged and thriving students. The opposite is also true: A stressed-out teacher cannot help but produce disengaged students. Every area of life—especially K-12 education—must recognize that the stresses of life and work will wear people down. This is often literally a life and death issue—with uncontrolled stress leading to a myriad of physical, mental health, and social problems. Yet, our cultural voices whisper, "Run just a little faster, work just a little harder." Another voice we hear is from our Christian culture that rightfully encourages a service orientation, but sometimes wrongly de-emphasizes the importance of healthy self-care as an essential tool for effective Christian service.

We must all try to resist those voices. Better yet, educate them. And that begins with educating ourselves. In our own settings, it is time to start a conversation about the need to restore health and well-being in our schools, our families, and throughout our communities. As we think about our work with schools and educators, there are two things that we deem as essential to this conversation:

1) principles for growth in the midst of stress and challenge; and 2) strategies for fostering well-being in our schools.

Principles for Growth

How can teachers and leaders grow in their well-being, especially amid ongoing stresses that show no signs of letting up (both those related to the job of educating, and also those pressed upon our schools by our societal and historical moment)? To develop a framework for well-being, we can consider the work of Dr. Martin Seligman, who was commissioned by the U.S. Army to study why up to 20 percent of soldiers who served three million tours of duty in Iraq and Afghanistan returned with post-traumatic stress disorder, or PTSD. While examining this area of deep concern, Seligman also discovered a small percentage of soldiers returned *stronger* from their combat experience (Seligman 2011). There are other examples of this growth journey, including Victor Frankl's experience in Auschwitz or Admiral Jim Stockdale's years as a prisoner of war in Vietnam.

This group, which Seligman described as experiencing post-traumatic growth, shared six key traits—which we can use as principles for educators—for growth in and through trauma and extreme challenge: 1) *resilient mindset;* 2) *activate your strengths;* 3) *"Circle of Five;"* 4) *energy (sleep, move, eat);* 5) *meaning/purpose;* and 6) *daily progress.* As we describe each one, we will also provide reflection questions for you to consider in your context.

1. Resilient Mindset

A resilient mindset is not thinking that circumstances will somehow magically get better. Instead, a scriptural view of a positive mindset hinges on verses like Romans 8:28, which promise that "all things work for good, for those who love the Lord." This refers to moral good—not that things simply work out for the better in our immediate circumstances. It means that our circumstances will produce good character and stronger faith. That's what a resilient mindset means in this context. We see this reflected in Romans 5:3-5 as well: "We also glory in our sufferings, because we know that suffering produces perseverance; perseverance, character; and character, hope. And hope does not put us to shame, because God's love has been poured out into our hearts through the Holy Spirit, who has been given to us."

In Christian schools, the starting point for our mindset is the truth of Scripture, which in turn forms the foundation of well-being in the midst of challenges. When we think about developing this principle for growth, educators can consider the following two questions. First, how do we nurture a resilient mindset, based in Scripture, for ourselves and our school staff? And second, when challenges come—as they inevitably will—how do we activate that mindset?

2. Activate Your Strengths

When we think about what we've learned from neuroscience, we know that a weakness is an area in the brain that is not highly developed. It has fewer synaptic clusters. When you stimulate that area, it may elevate for a short period, but there's nothing supporting it to sustain that growth. By way of contrast, when you activate a strength, it is reinforced by the web of neurons that surround it. The development of one strength is supported by others. In most cases, activating our strengths can work to make our weaknesses irrelevant. There is also a physiological benefit to activating your strengths. When they are activated, your body releases dopamine, the pleasure and joy hormone. When you become so absorbed in what you're doing, your body releases endorphins, the endurance or runner's high hormone. These are key to a state of well-being and a reduction of stress, which triggers the cortisol hormone.

Often, adults need to rediscover their own strengths. Children possess a quality of curiosity that allows them to master incredible skills before going to school. We take walking and talking for granted, but imagine if we kept that learning capacity through life. NASA developed an assessment in the 1960s to select the best and brightest for the space program (Land 1993). The evaluation measured creativity, and mirrored the kind of creativity found in children. George Land, the creator of the assessment, administered it to 1,600 preschool children. Ninety-eight percent tested as geniuses. He followed these students for another ten years, and they retook the assessment. The number of kids who kept that level of creativity dropped to 12 percent. Land followed these students into adulthood, and fifteen years later, read-ministered the assessment and the percentage dropped to two percent (Land's team also tested 280,000 adults, and the percentage for that large sample was also two percent). The point is that by adulthood, most of us have lost the ability and joy of expressing our best selves.

Discovering and developing those innate capacities and traits provides a map to personal growth, intrinsic happiness, and reclaiming some of the characteristics God gave us at birth. When we think about developing this principle for growth, educators can consider the following two questions. First, how do we create a culture that allows ourselves and our school staff to explore our strengths, and activate those to make improvements? And second, how can we increase time and resources for adults to "play"—to re-develop their creativity and joy in their work?

3. "Circle of Five"

Part of the resilience or the growth found in soldiers returning from the war was tied to their having a tight network of relationships. This is the "Circle of Five"—the five key relationships in your life that provide buoyancy, balance, and hold you to your better self. The research is clear: We need to have five vital, active relationships to maintain happiness and get through challenging times. Who could you call at two in the morning and would pick up the phone and be there for you? Who would hold you to your best self? Who would you feel comfortable speaking truth to you, even if you didn't want to hear it?

Gallup has pointed out that we need a close colleague, a friend at work (Mann 2018). A person who does not have a close colleague or friend at work is 60 percent more likely to leave that place of employment than those who have that relationship. Research also shows that people have, on average, one and a half trusted relationships. You may have heard of a "loneliness epidemic." The COVID-19 pandemic has exposed the harm of loneliness; a recent Kaiser Family Foundation report found that in January 2021, 41 percent of adults reported symptoms of anxiety or depressive disorder, compared to 11 percent the year prior (Panchal et al. 2021).

Meaningful social connections at work, and outside of work, are key to well-being and post-traumatic growth. Social connection is restorative, while isolation contributes to poor mental health. When we think about developing this principle for growth, educators can consider the following questions. First, how do we nurture meaningful social connections for ourselves and our school staff? Do we allow time for social engagement, celebration, and support? Second, how can we reduce the isolation of leaders and teachers through policies and practices around collaboration, shared space, co-teaching, and others?

4. Energy (Sleep, Move, Eat)

During times of challenge, we often turn to unhealthy coping behaviors to manage stress such as comfort food, or becoming sedentary. These are all unhealthy coping behaviors that impede sleep, impede recovery, and put us on a vicious cycle of becoming more and more depleted each day. Life's distractions, long days of stress, watching screens before going to bed, and other interferences make it difficult to get a good night's sleep. The best place to start in thinking about this is to conduct a sleep audit.

How many hours of sleep do you get? If you're getting less than seven hours a night, you are sleep deprived, along with 70 percent of our nation. How consistent are you with your sleep routine? It's not just enough to sleep, but consistency matters because your body depends on routine and rhythm. In the book *WHOLE: What*

Teachers Need to Help Students Thrive (Miller et al. 2020) there is a chapter called "Waking the Dead." It addresses the challenge of a lack of sleep in schools and how it hinders student performance. If an entire school got a week's worth of consistent sleep, it could indeed transform them. Whatever amount of sleep you are currently getting should be slowly increased another thirty minutes to an hour, while decreasing your screen time before bed.

Getting enough rest doesn't just mean enough sleep at night, though that is essential. It's also important to take breaks during the day. You can't run a marathon like a sprint. Teachers are "on" all day long. That is simply not sustainable. New research confirms that we all have a daily work rhythm that is similar to our sleep rhythm at night. Your brain maxes out at 90 minutes of cognitive load (as in teaching) before it has to rest. Otherwise, you damage it, like pulling a muscle. Your brain won't signal the pain because it has no nerve endings. You need a full 15- to 30-minute break when you rest, which doesn't mean simply switching tasks. This means a walk outside, quiet contemplation or prayer, or a power nap—and always drinking a large glass of water on your break.

Similarly, we need to take our Sabbath seriously. According to A. J. Swoboda, in his book, *Subversive Sabbath* (2018), Americans have "Sabbath amnesia." And, the result of that "is that we have become perhaps the most emotionally exhausted, psychologically overworked, spiritually malnourished people in history." Taking one full day a week for rest, reflection, family, and worship represents an ancient and still essential recalibrating of our relationship to time and work. Recent research has demonstrated that Sabbath keeping has a clear relationship with the wellness of Christian school communities, including lower frequencies of educator burnout, higher levels of church involvement, and greater fellowship with family and church members (Lee, Djita, and Cheng 2021).

Improving physical health may be a catalyst for the other disciplines. There are proven practices that will help shift to healthier

Taking one full day a week for rest, reflection, family, and worship represents an ancient and still essential recalibrating of our relationship to time and work.

behaviors. For example, daily exercise is a great habit. However, what's even better is incorporating movement throughout the day. NASA took this approach to develop a way for astronauts to counteract the adverse effects of weightlessness in space. NASA calls adding movement throughout the day "NEAT." It stands for non-exercise activity thermogenesis (Levine 2022). Examples include parking at the end of a parking lot and walking to a building, or using the stairs versus an elevator. Leaving 15 minutes between meetings and using that time to do a quick series of exercises, as well as drink a glass of water, will add up to big benefits by the end of every day. This kind of movement gets the blood flowing enough to oxygenate the brain and flush some of the cortisol (stress) out of the body.

Finally, the difficult truth is that losing weight should be a by-product of enjoying a healthier life. The challenge with this is that the norm set by the food industry for a balanced diet is harming us. Your primary enemy begins with sugar in all forms. That includes foods high in carbohydrates and sugar slipped into all processed food. The amount of sugar in food is one area the food industry cleverly disguises, killing us for lack of knowledge and discipline. We need to start slowly and wean ourselves off sugar, which is an addictive substance (it activates a dopamine release in the nucleus accumbens part of our brain—just like cocaine and heroin). An effective strategy to use is to focus on what to add to your diet, such as fiber from whole foods; by adding in healthy foods, this often results in eating less refined sugar, salt, and unhealthy fats. By starting to do something positive with our diets, we may find it easier to eliminate the negative behaviors.

When we think about developing this principle for growth, educators can consider the following two questions. First, how do we provide the space, time, and resources for ourselves and our school staff to engage in healthy behaviors of rest, physical activity, and nutritious eating? And second, how might our cramped daily schedules, physical spaces that lack light or air circulation, and other factors be negatively impacting our ability to be physically healthy in our schools?

5. Meaning/Purpose

One of the traits that the soldiers with post-traumatic growth had is meaning in their life. There was something bigger, and beyond them, they lived for. The origin of this research comes from a psychologist by the name of Victor Frankl who was a prisoner of war in Auschwitz. He observed the difference between those who survived and those who died. To summarize, he found that those who did not survive had the kind of optimistic thinking that we see in self-help books, as in "the world will somehow get better if I just think it's going to get better."

By contrast, those who survived found meaning. They lived for something beyond themselves and bigger than themselves. Victor Frankel's observations' underlying premise is that if you believe the world has a purpose and that you have free will, you have agency. In other words, you can choose to interpret your circumstances in light of that purpose. Thus, having meaning and purpose entails having a framework for interpreting the work you are doing—in your current context and your circumstances—in light of something beyond you, something bigger than you. Your faith and the Christian philosophy of your school's education is the perfect place to recenter yourself and find meaning for your work.

When we think about developing this principle for growth, educators can consider the following two questions. First, as a team, how do we focus as much (or more) on our "why" than our "how"—meaning our mission, instead of just our practices? And second, when we become bogged down in the daily weeds and challenges, how can we refocus on the deep meaning of our work as Christian educators?

6. Daily Progress

The final principle is a sense of accomplishment that must be cultivated daily. This principle involves the idea of marginal gains, which when you factor in the "magic" of compound interest, add up to tremendous benefit over time. This trait goes back again to mindset. Are you looking for signs of progress? What do you measure progress by? In the current uncertain conditions, what we used to measure may no longer provide a measure of success or progress. We must look for new metrics of success and different metrics for progress.

The secret to making progress begins with this principle: Start small but stay consistent. Investing in healthy habits is like compound interest or seed sown in good soil. This principle will work with gradually increasing the number of sit-ups, servings of vegetables, or additional minutes of sleep we get each night. Starting slow and working up to a wellness target is the best way to ensure success. Focusing on the process, not the outcome, is a subtle shift. But research tells us that we're less likely to quit, and more likely to reach our goals, if we prioritize putting a gradual process into place versus just running all out at the target.

When we think about developing this principle for growth, educators can consider the following two questions. First, how do we recognize and reward daily accomplishments of ourselves and our teams, versus just big or splashy achievements? And second, how can we focus more on the daily process of working toward wellness in our own lives and our schools, versus just the big (and often seemingly unattainable) goals like losing twenty pounds or exercising thirty minutes a day?

Strategies for Fostering Well-Being

In the Christian world, we talk a great deal about personal responsibility. And it is true that people are both responsible and accountable for the decisions they make in every area of life. It is crucial for individuals to be responsible for taking steps toward their own health and well-being in the workplace. But there is also a profound impact that the work culture and environment have on an employee's ability to make positive health choices that will enable them to thrive in the workplace and at home. In the reflection questions offered in this chapter, we have hinted that the workplace culture as much influences well-being as an individual's choices. James 2:16 says that when a Christian says to a person in need, "'Go in peace; keep warm and well fed,' but does nothing about their physical needs, what good is it?" The same can be said about caring for the well-being of teachers and leaders in our schools.

When it comes to supporting teacher well-being in Christian schools, it is important for every school leader to ask themselves this question: *Is the culture and environment of our school an asset or a detriment to the well-being of the teachers and leaders who serve our Christ-centered mission?* Particularly for teachers, what hinders their well-being the most is not the act of teaching itself. Rather, the greatest barrier to teacher health and well-being comes from managing the expectations of parents, administrators, and community. In an article from *EdWeek* entitled "Teachers Are Not OK, Even Though We Need Them to Be," 42 percent of teachers said administrators had not made any effort to help relieve their stress, and about 20 percent said whatever their administrators had tried didn't help. But only two percent didn't think there was anything that their schools could do to help—which means there is definitely room for improvement in supporting school staff and creating school cultures that support wellness (Will 2021).

Some of the expectations that present the greatest challenge to teacher well-being are in the roles of *the responder* and *the role model*. Let's look at each of these roles and how school leaders can support teacher well-being within each context.

Responders Need Routines

Christian teachers are leaders of the learning experiences in their classroom, but they are also function as responders. Much like a nurse on a hospital floor, they are tasked with responding to the needs of their individual students. In order to fulfill the responder aspect of teaching, they often feel expected to do little extras on their personal time and they feel the pressure to be in "on and respond" mode most of the time.

For most people, making good health decisions would not be hard if those decisions did not have to be made on such a daily, hourly, and even moment-by-moment basis. Because the sheer volume of decisions made each day in response to student needs is mentally exhausting, little energy is left for making and executing the decisions around health and well-being. The more daily health habits that can be incorporated into the daily routine, the better chance teachers will have of living well within the responder role.

As a school leader, what measures have you taken to protect your teachers' before- and after-work routines, given that they operate in the responder mode most of the day? The chart below will help you think through the answers to this question.

Well-Being Issue	Questions for School Leaders
Work commitments before or after school hours disrupt adults' health routines.	What are your criteria for determining if an issue is important enough to disrupt teachers' before- and after-work routines? Of leaders? Do you have other options for addressing pressing issues?

Well-Being Issue	Questions for School Leaders
Parent/student communications outside of school hours disrupt health routines.	In what ways have you supported limits of teacher and leader access after-hours?
	How have you clearly communicated to parents expectations regarding accessibility and responsiveness of staff outside of business hours?
	Have you clearly defined what an "emergency" is and is not, and how the school leadership will handle repeated inappropriate "emergency" communications?

Role Models Need Resources

Christian teachers are leaders of the learning experience in their classrooms, but they also serve as role models of Christian living to the students in their school. In order to fulfill the role model aspect of their work, teachers often feel expected to walk the talk and be consistently good ambassadors for Christ to their students. They often forget that attending to their body and mind, as well as spirit, are part of that. Churches and Christian schools often focus on providing resources for spiritual well-being, while resources for physical and mental well-being are overlooked. Helping teachers be role models for Christian living requires resources beyond just the spiritual.

As a school leader, what help are you providing to assist teachers in becoming positive role models for students in body, mind, and spirit? The chart on the next page will help you think through the answers to this question.

Teacher Well-Being Issue	Questions for School Leaders
Teachers who have no coverage to attend to basic biological functions during the workday will be less able to serve their students well and send a powerful message to their students about the role of the body and health in the Christian life.	Do the teachers in your school attend to their basic biological functions (eating lunch, using the restroom, taking a break or a walk outside) on the fly or is there a provision to perform these activities regularly with a minimum of interruptions? How might you utilize school staff and parent volunteers to add support to this teacher well-being issue?
Teachers who do not perceive a level of safety when dealing with problematic mental, emotional, or relational issues will be less likely to seek help and will send a powerful message to their students about the management of thoughts, feelings, and relationships in the Christian life.	Do your teachers have access to a resource for biblical counseling outside of the school (or outside of the church affiliated with the school, if applicable) that is associated with their employment? If biblical counseling in a church-sponsored school is offered to teachers through that church, what provisions are in place to protect their privacy as employees beyond the privacy provisions for the general congregation? What referrals or processes does your school have in place for employees who may need professional mental health evaluation and perhaps treatment?

Scripture reminds us, "And masters, treat your servants considerately. Be fair with them. Don't forget for a minute that you, too, serve a Master—God in heaven" (Col. 4:1, MSG). As servants of Christ, we can be happy that our Master goes far beyond being considerate and fair, as He equips and enables us in our service. Instead, He blesses us abundantly. When it comes to teacher well-being, what can you do to bless and serve those who serve the mission of your Christian school?

Putting It All Together

Christian schools developed multiple strategies to support well-being during the COVID-19 pandemic, like extra staffing and aides, counseling resources, partnerships with outside wellness groups, additional time off or mental health days, reducing meetings, reworking master schedules to allow more prep time, and revamping spaces for rest and recharging (Swaner and Lee 2020). The question is whether they will systemize these and other practices both now and in the future to create cultures of wellness.

Jesus states the risk of not building on a firm foundation in Matthew 7. God loves us and wants us to have a foundation of physical and emotional resiliency built on the truth of His Word. We can then bring this life to our schools, colleagues, and students, who will then go out and influence their families and affect their communities for the good.

Part 3:
Programs and Practices

Core Components of Student Care
Cara Dixon, *Growth Minded Counseling and Consulting*

Christian schools vary widely in their resources, personnel, and student demographics. The reality is that no two Christian schools, though they may be similar in many aspects, are exactly alike. In the U.S., there are also no national or otherwise unified standards to guide care for students with mental health needs in private schools. Taken together, this means that who addresses mental health needs, and how they do it, will look different from school to school.

However, research and best practice in school mental health suggests that there are core components that should be in place in schools, which in turn will enable educators to fulfill their duty of caring for students with various mental health needs. This chapter will outline several of these components: the school's philosophy and needs assessment related to mental health, which form the premise for mental health care; school policies and procedures, which shape the practice of mental health care; and school and external teams, which comprise the people who will engage in providing mental health care.

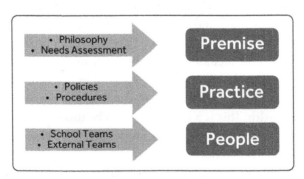

The Premise for Care: Philosophy and Needs Assessment

Chapter 1 briefly covered the importance of articulating a philosophy for how your school approaches mental health needs. The philosophy statement, which should align with the school's overall mission, can be written in a few sentences. For example:

> "At New Life Christian School, we care holistically for students so they can flourish in all that God has designed them to be, in and through Christ (Eph. 2:10). This includes intentionally addressing students' emotional well-being and mental health through best practices in prevention, support, and intervention, in collaboration with families, pastoral staff, and mental health professionals."

There may be an added statement that aligns with specific values the school strives to achieve in student life, such as interdependence, character development, resilience, and so forth. Consider including scriptural references that are foundational to the specific philosophy your school is articulating.

It is important that the vision statement not be created unilaterally by school leadership, but rather by a group or committee that also includes select teachers, the school nurse, any counseling and resource staff, parents, and area mental health professionals who are trusted and in your relational circle (if yours is a church-sponsored school, be sure to include representation from the pastoral staff). Task the group with collaboratively researching, discussing, and then prayerfully drafting your school's philosophy and overall approach to mental health. This is a key step not to be missed, as philosophy statements provide the foundation for designing, implementing, and evaluating actual practice.

Along with developing a philosophy statement, Chapter 1 discussed the importance of conducting a self-audit. This needs assessment effort should gauge student mental health concerns in your school, as well as examine how the leadership team, teachers, and others address those needs at the present moment. It is important to note that the school may already have existing data that can be used in this process, such as demographic information, attendance, visits to the nurse, retention measures from the previous year, or frequency of mental health-related incidents. There are also ready-made counseling needs assessments available online that can be used to gather data about mental health needs.

In addition to data on prevalence of mental health concerns, developing a process or flowchart of how mental health needs are *actually* handled at the school (in real practice, versus the ideal or as they're supposed to) will help in assessing where bottlenecks, pain points, and other areas of concern may lie. And finally, be sure to research the laws and requirements of your state (where applicable), the requirements of the school's insurance carrier, and any other legal or liability obligations the school may have. Once the information is gathered and organized, it can be used in the development or refinement of programs, policies and procedures, teams and care networks, and budgets and resource allocation.

Taken together, a well-articulated philosophy of care for students, coupled with a solid needs assessment that is done annually, will help provide a solid foundation—or premise—for meeting the well-being and mental health needs of students in your school. And it is upon this foundation that the actual practice of care can be built, through clear policies and procedures that are aligned with best practice in school mental health.

The Practice of Care: Policies and Procedures

Policies and procedures are the backbone of operational practices. They are a clearly defined set of guidelines that outline how an institution strategically approaches situations to promote, enforce, and maintain positive outcomes. Policies and procedures not only promote the well-being of students, but also inform school staff and parents of how mental health concerns should be handled, as well as provide safeguards and protect the school in terms of liability. It's helpful to think of policies and procedures like the beams behind a wall: Though they are not visible to the casual observer, the wall cannot stand without them. Without effective policies and procedures, operations will go unsupported and eventually crumble under pressure, just like a wall without a beam.

Writing Policies and Procedures

Creating policies and procedures is a process, and one that should involve input from all stakeholders and reflect best practice. The school likely has policies and procedures for other operational practices, so policies and procedures pertaining to mental health might fall under existing headings for student support or health services in the school's overall policy manual. If the school does not have a single, unified operational manual, then policies and procedures around student mental health might compose their own smaller manual.

Policies usually consist of headings and subheadings. The headings are broad operational points that bracket a series of more descriptive policies connected to the heading. They should be relevant to the specific population in the school, as per the needs assessment data. Some examples of headings are listed below:

1. Communication
2. Documentation
3. System Operation
4. Mandated Reporting
5. Emergency Management
6. Quality Improvement
7. Cultural Considerations in Student Mental Health
8. Support Plans
9. Student Support Files

Under each heading should be a series of policies that create limits and regulations that are important to upholding operations. The procedures under each policy explain, step-by-step, how that policy should be carried out.

SAMPLE POLICY. Below is an example of a policy heading, with policy subheadings and procedures following.

1. Communication

1.1 Confidential Communication

Policy: This policy ensures that all communication adheres to HIPPA and FERPA laws that protect the confidentiality of individuals with regard to health information or identification.

Procedure:

    a. All records, health information, or student reports with identifying information will be kept locked in a file cabinet in a locked room.

    b. Email communication regarding student health related concerns will be limited to scheduling, or a one- to two-sentence follow-up with only the first name or initials of the individual.

    c. Person-to-person communication regarding student health is limited to confidential space of and should not occur in hallways, classrooms, or other spaces that are not protected.

1.2 Intra-School Communication about Mental Health Concerns

Policy: This policy is in place to promote appropriate times and spaces for communication about a student's mental health, and to streamline all mental health concerns in a consistent direction and ensure maximum support for any issue that is presented.

Procedure:

    a. If a student need or mental health concern arises, then a referral form should be filled out and submitted to the designated mental health point person, with a request for follow up.

    b. Follow-up on mental health concerns after the referral form is submitted should occur no later than 48 hours after being submitted.

    c. Student needs or mental health concerns can be discussed during prearranged student support meetings, or in scheduled confidential offices with the intention of referral to the support team, or follow-up on interventions.

Additional policies under the subheading of Communication might include Faculty-to-Parent Communication, School Staff to Outside Provider Communication, and so forth.

When policies and procedures are initially put into place, it is important to have adequate training for staff, enforcement strategies, and an evaluation period to ensure effectiveness. There will also likely be a period where modifications are necessary, before policies (again, like wall beams) come to a place where they are "settled." If a new policy needs to be implemented, the process should be led by the administrative team and include a thorough review to make sure there is enough supporting evidence to formally establish the policy. Finally, it is best practice to evaluate policies on an annual basis. Policies and procedures should be a part of the larger annual review process of all mental health system functions. In their *Guidelines for a*

Student Support Component, the Summits Initiative at UCLA (2002) includes the following indicators for evaluation and reassessment, to ensure quality for support services in schools:

- Systems and interventions are monitored and improved as necessary.

- Programs and services constitute a comprehensive, multifaceted continuum.

- Interveners have appropriate knowledge and skills for their roles and functions and provide guidance for continuing professional development.

- School-owned programs and services are coordinated and integrated.

- School-owned programs and services are connected to home and community resources.

- Programs and services are integrated with instructional and governance/management components at schools.

- Program/services are available, accessible, and appealing.

- Empirically supported interventions are used when applicable.

- Differences among students/families are appropriately accounted for (e.g., diversity, disability, developmental levels, motivational levels, strengths, weaknesses).

- Legal considerations are appropriately accounted for (e.g., mandated services; mandated reporting and its consequences).

- Ethical issues are appropriately accounted for (e.g., privacy and confidentiality; coercion).

- Contexts for intervention are appropriate (e.g., office; clinic; classroom; home).

In addition to assessing policies and procedures against standards and indicators like the previous list, an annual review process may also include data collection on these policies and procedures to formally demonstrate their effectiveness. This can include both short- and long-term outcome data, which in turn should be reported to stakeholders and used to enhance future interventions.

Documentation and Confidentiality

Documenting the mental health needs of students, and the school's responses to those needs, is crucial in the school setting. First, documentation enables there to be a record and history, which will be essential for future situations or symptoms that present with a given student. Without excellent documentation, school staff will waste invaluable time starting over each time a student presents a need. This is particularly dangerous in times of crisis, which need to be de-escalated and addressed as quickly as possible. If the case history is documented and appropriately filed, it will not only save a lot of time, but also help staff to make the most informed decisions in the current moment of need. Documentation is also important in that it maintains a consistent record of interventions so that those involved currently or in the future are all on the same page. It shows interventions, tracking, progress, and other variables that were considered. It is essential with mental health concerns to foster a unified approach and have information that is accessible to the team providing care for the student, so that decisions can be consistent and informed.

Finally, documentation provides data if needed to justify a school's decisions, or demonstrate a clear course of action. For example, if there are grounds for a student's dismissal, the file may provide evidence of minimal or no progress, given what the school could provide. This would allow the school to make a decision that was based on data and provide a clear representation of how the school addressed the case within that context. It may help in demonstrating that a school is not fit to provide for the need adequately with available resources and can provide grounds for demonstrating how another setting may more appropriately fit the student's need. Moreover, if documentation is needed for a court case or legal reasons, good documentation will ensure that the school will not be scrambling at the last minute to put something together. Documentation is a way to demonstrate the school staff's diligence with each concern that has arisen.

The core method of documentation is the student case file. This file should contain documents such as intake forms, progress notes from any interaction with the student, the support plan for the student (Chapter 8 covers support plans in detail), release forms signed by parents or guardians to speak with outside providers (see the sample provided in the Resources section of this monograph), doctor's notes or letters provided to the school, and any relevant communication (email or written, or notes made on phone calls) from parents, providers, teachers, other school staff, and the student, as applicable.

It is important to note that, just like health data, the student mental health case file is protected under various federal laws and legislation. Best practices for secure storage and should be followed by schools. Practically speaking, this should include storing student case files with mental health documentation separately from academic and health files. While it is permissible (even advisable) to make a mark or notation on academic and health files that a mental health case file exists for the student, no documentation relative to mental health may be stored outside of the designated file. All case files should be "double locked," meaning they are placed in a locked filing cabinet, which itself is kept in a locked room or office (which is monitored if/when unlocked); only designated school staff should have access to the files. Since many schools now keep electronic documents as well (e.g., emails, behavioral notes in student information systems), it is important to ensure that policies and procedures are in place for keeping electronic files as secure—if not more secure—than physical records.

Additionally, schools need to ensure the maintenance of confidentiality while handling or discussing student cases. For example, if emailing regarding a student, there should be no identifying information in emails (and names should be identified by either first name or initials, not the student's full name). All discussions about student cases should occur in specific spaces identified as confidential, and notes from student support meetings should be shredded or put in the same locked filing cabinet as student case files. It is also important to have a written confidentiality policy that is reviewed with students, families, and school staff. The policy should state that all documentation and the information it contains is kept strictly confidential unless: 1) the student is at risk of harm; 2) it is determined that another person is at risk of harm; and/or 3) there is a court mandate. Finally, student plans and other forms contained with the student file should not be copied or provided to anyone either within or outside of the school without written consent by the parent or guardian.

The People Who Care: Intervention Teams

Can you imagine fishing with just your hands? Fish are slippery, fast, and sporadic. In contrast, nets provide a way for multiple fish to be caught and held firmly without the risk of sliding from one's grasp. It is the job of organizations that lead multiple people, especially children, to have a well-developed design, or system, to catch and hold students that may be slipping. Since schools have the responsibility for many children, tending to one individual with one tool at a time without a system (or net made up of many efforts that are woven well together) leaves a lot of individuals without care, or compromised care at best. In the school context, intervention teams provide the safety net for students when it comes to mental health.

Creating such a net in schools takes intentionality and planning. It is important to note that many Christian schools do not have the resources for a full-time, licensed professional counselor or social worker—which makes the creation of a net all the more important. This must include identifying the roles and responsibilities of individuals involved in student supports, both in and outside of school. Having solid resources, and roles and responsibilities thought out ahead of time, will weave together each effort into a tightly knit network that can hold many students without having any slip through holes in the system. For the purposes of this chapter, intervention teams can be divided into two categories: those inside the school, and those external to the school.

Support Teams in the School

There are two teams that are critical to develop in the school. The first is a Student Support Team and the second is a Crisis Intervention Team. There could be crossover of individuals that serve on both teams, but individuals' functions on the team to which they are assigned is important to consider. The Student Support Team should be comprised of administrators or those in leadership roles at the school. This team is designed to implement intentional interventions, track effectiveness, and communicate with mental health professionals, students, and families. A sample roster for a Student Support Team, with roles and responsibilities, is provided below.

Job Titles	Team Roles	Responsibilities
Point Person #1 **Point Person #2 (serves as back-up to #1)** These roles are often fulfilled by administrators like a school counselor or a dean of students.	• Case Management • Program Development • Lead in meetings	• Organize team meetings • Manage referrals and student support files • Documentation • Develop and implement student support plans (discussed in Chapter 8) • Family contact to schedule meetings • Coordinating supports in and out of school • Incorporate mental health speakers, groups, or other preventative approaches for education and skills training

Job Titles	Team Roles	Responsibilities
Administrative Lead This role is often fulfilled by a principal (upper and lower school).	• Administrative (policy enforcement, compliance, official letters, data collection)	• Attend Behavior Support Plan Meetings • Family contact (e.g., draft/write letters) • Enforce referral system to manage concerns • Managing faculty compliance with support interventions • Collect data on effectiveness of system and analyze to make modifications annually
Health Lead This role is typically fulfilled by the school nurse.	• Consultation regarding health requirements, perspectives, and approaches	• Provide health-related data and education to incorporate into each case • Monitor health needs and refer to Student Support Team if the needs present with mental health symptoms
Student Life Representatives These roles are often filled by learning support staff, guidance staff, residential life directors (if applicable), chaplains, campus pastors, and teachers.	• Intervention implementation	• Implement interventions and accommodations as indicated on support plan • Data collection for support plan, which provides progress updates to Point Person • Reporting information that is relevant to the case at Student Support Team meetings, either in advance (to the Point Person) or at meetings

The Crisis Team is a group of designated individuals who are trained to respond to crisis. A crisis team must be developed in advance, because "effective crisis management does not start with the critical incident response" (Reeves, Brock, and Cowan, 2008). There is extensive literature and best practice protocols that are available to guide the development of this team. [See Chapter 9, which addresses crisis response in the school setting.] Crisis can be defined simply as an incident or situation that is dangerous or disruptive, whether to the individual student, other students, school staff, or the school as a whole. There are times when a crisis is obvious in nature thus responded to immediately, and instances when an individual is in distress to a situation that may not appear particularly distressing. Initial assessment to determine whether it's a crisis situation can include questions like:

- Is the situation dangerous or disruptive?
- Is the individual's ability to problem solve or cope seriously disrupted?
- Is there a possibility of imminent harm in the individual's environment either at school, at home, or in the community?
- Is this a situation that needs to be reported as the responsibility of mandated reporters?

For all in-school intervention teams, knowledge of school policies and procedures related to mental health is an absolute requirement. This includes ethical standards for communication between and among team members when it comes to confidentiality, including confining discussion about student cases to confidential spaces, obtaining signed consent before discussing or releasing information, and ensuring that emails do not contain confidential information, including students' full names.

Staff training is also essential for any individual serving on an intervention team and should be provided by a mental health professional on topics such as recognizing signs of distress, de-escalating crisis, behavior support plans, emergency management protocols, prevention approaches, and triage. Training for teams should be planned, implemented, and evaluated annually, and should be part of a larger training program for all school staff (on such topics as identifying signs of sexual abuse, mandated reporting training, school policies and procedures related to mental health, and basic crisis response).

Support Teams Outside of School

It is equally important to have a support team developed outside of the school as it is to have one inside the school. This external team can include counselors, psychologists, psychiatrists, behavior specialists, neurologists, primary care physicians, support groups, case managers, autism services, hospitals, partial hospitals, and intensive outpatient services. A thorough research and relationship building process is recommended in order to design an effective network outside of the school. While this process should lead to the production of a list of names of mental health providers or services in the area, this team of individuals is not just the list itself. Rather, outside providers and services should be intentionally woven into the net of the school student support system.

The school point person should collect information about each practitioner or service and get to know the people. This may look like talking to them in person, seeing the places that they practice, and getting to know their process and style. Some steps to consider during the initial contact phone call or meeting include:

1. Asking about the services provided (take brochures or cards to have for families).
2. Asking about credentials, experience, and how long they have been in practice.
3. Asking about specialties (i.e., families, teens, eating disorders, substance abuse, self-harm).
4. Noting the therapeutic modalities and evidenced-based practices that are used.
5. Gathering information on the referral process, and asking

how long it takes between the initial phone call and the
first appointment.
6. Discussing collaboration efforts and how much time is
allotted for collaboration with schools.
7. Asking if services include programs, trainings, or speaking
engagements, including a list of topics.
8. Asking how they approach spirituality and faith-based
disclosures.
9. Discussing payment and whether they take insurance.
10. Describing the mission and values of the school.
11. Explaining the system and process at the school to find out
if this would be a match with their services.

The purpose of this encounter is more than asking questions—it
is developing a rapport in order to explore an ongoing professional
relationship to best serve students and families. If the provider or
program is not a good fit, thank them for their time and explore
another provider to fill the spot. If the initial contact is successful
and the provider appears to be a good fit, it is recommended that
another time to talk is arranged to nurture the connection. Again,
the goal is not just to create a referral list; the goal is to build bridges
with mental health professionals and programs in the community,
so that when situations at the school arise, relationships with the
outside support team is already established.

Students and Parents: Part of the Team

While they do not formally serve on either internal or external
intervention teams, students and their parents (or guardians) are critical
team players in order for any intervention strategy to be developed
and implemented successfully. Forging effective partnerships with
students and their parents includes establishing boundaries, clear
communication, and proactive outreach.

My father, a retired research psychologist at the University of

Pennsylvania, wisely reminds me that for many students, abstract thinking and problem solving abilities are still forming. They are developing executive cognitive functioning skills and as such, it is a challenge to think outside of the present moment. Having students involved in proactive discussion, strategizing, and evaluation of interventions creates fertile ground for modeling executive functioning skills and promoting agency.

When it comes to relationships with parents, the school cannot control parents' responses, but clear communication with a set plan, boundaries, and intentional strategies can help to limit reactive responses and channel communication in a direction towards positive growth and change. Troubleshooting among the support team when there are breakdowns or concerns in school relationships is key, whether parents are not communicating well, do not think there is a problem (or are contributing to the problem), or want something that goes against school policy. Parents are an enormous resource and their support is needed for successful reinforcement of interventions strategies in the home environment and to provide resources for additional supports; it is worth the time and effort to develop positive relationships, boundaries, and communication with parents, which will benefit the student, the family, and the school support teams as they journey together toward greater wholeness and well-being.

Putting It All Together: The Need for a System

This chapter outlined several core components of caring well for students' mental health needs. This starts with the school's philosophy and needs assessment related to mental health, which form the premise for mental health care. It also must include school policies and procedures, which shape the practice of mental health care. And finally, it includes school and external teams, which comprise the people who will engage in providing mental health care.

Putting all of these components together successfully and in an ordered fashion requires another step—organizing them into a well-designed system, so that decisions around student care are not "one-off" but rather run on a predetermined track that is created collaboratively with mental health professionals and employs best practices. In Chapter 8, we provide suggestions for developing such a system in private Christian schools, thereby ensuring that the essential components of care work together efficiently, consistently, and effectively toward the desired result of enhanced student well-being and growth.

Systematizing Support in Christian Schools
Cara Dixon, *Growth Minded Counseling and Consulting*
Charlotte Marshall Powell, *Barna Group*

Imagine that a middle school student bursts into tears during an English midterm. The teacher is unable to figure out what is causing the situation, as the student—now sobbing uncontrollably—cannot respond to the teacher's questions. Unable to calm the student down, and with the situation quickly becoming disruptive to the entire class, the teacher asks another student to escort the first to the principal's office. The teacher then calls ahead to let the office know that the student is en route.

As an administrator, what thoughts go through your mind when you get the call? What runs through your mind as the student is about to arrive at your office? At this point, the possibilities are many. Was the student just unprepared for the exam and is upset at the likelihood of a failing grade? Does the student have a history of test anxiety, and do you need to consider putting supports in place for the student during midterms? Is there something difficult going on at home that is making focusing on the exam impossible for the student? Is the student being bullied during the study hall immediately following the English class? Did the student's best friend post something on social media the night before about committing suicide, and the student is worried because the friend is absent from school today? Or, is the crying student on the way to your office the one who's thinking of committing self harm? With these and other possible scenarios looming, and the student about to round the corner into your office, how do you know what to do next?

This chapter is intended to help Christian school staff identify the level of severity of students' mental health needs, and then recognize how to respond appropriately. To accomplish this, we propose using a system of *tiers*—or levels—of severity and response. A tiered system is not a unique approach to this book; in fact, it is widely recognized as best practice in the field of school-based mental health. Before laying out our own tier-based system for the Christian school, which we have used with success at multiple schools and that is adaptable to your own setting, we will provide a rationale for employing a tiered system.

Why a Tiered System?

Have you ever watched a kids' soccer game—not elementary kids, but preschool-aged? Typically, the preschoolers flock together, running back and forth on the field, just following the ball. The whole team's efforts are futile, as the kids are exhausted quickly and the ball struggles to make progress in any direction, let alone get to the goal. It can be hard to watch, especially if you know that with defined positions and responsibilities (i.e. offense, middies, and defense), the players would stay in their zones and would be ready for their specific role when the ball came to them.

Ideally, this is the way mental health needs should be handled in Christian schools—through an organized *system*. In such a system, the goal is clearly defined, a strategy for achieving that goal is established, and the whole team knows their individual roles and responsibilities to keep the ball moving in the right direction. The benefits of a system are many:

- A system creates a *unified approach*, which allows others inside and outside of the school to understand students' needs and respond efficiently. For example, parents of a student with a mental health concern do not receive one answer from the principal, another from the school nurse, and yet another from their child's teacher; rather, all school staff are on the same page.

- A system provides a *common language*, or a means to communicate strategies that have already been thought out, for all involved. This shared understanding of tactics, roles, and responsibilities bypasses the need to spend a lot of time to rehash philosophy and larger strategy every time a student need arises.

- A system positions the school staff in a *proactive stance*, meaning that they are prepared to handle any situation at any time, without having to devise strategies afresh in the moment. This helps to not only relieve the anxiety that staff often feel (for example, in helping a student who is in crisis), but also ensures that student needs are properly managed with due diligence (which is key not only for caring well for students, but also ensuring safety and mitigating liability).

Over the past ten years there has been a growing body of literature on the positive impact of having a system in schools to guide mental health assessment and intervention. There are likely several reasons for this. First, schools are often a first point of contact for detecting emotional, behavioral, or social concerns. Secondly, school-age children are at a critical point in their development, where intervening with appropriate support can yield significant growth—rather than further development of patterns of dysfunction. Finally, research has identified positive outcomes in schools that have implemented evidenced-based systems (Haggard et al. 2007).

The Multi-Tiered System of Supports (MTSS)

The most common system in schools that has been instrumental in creating a continuum of care for mental health concerns is Multi-Tiered System of Supports (MTSS). MTSS is an umbrella term for systems that involve "prevention and wellness promotion, universal screening for behavioral and academic barriers to learning, implementing evidenced-based interventions that increased in intensity as needed, monitoring the ongoing progress of students in response to implemented interventions, and engaging in systematic decision making about programing and services needed for students based upon specific student outcome data" (Vaillancourt et al. 2016, 1). Many educators and schools are familiar with Response-To-Intervention (RTI), which is a prime example of an MTSS and is an evidenced-based approach that has produced positive outcomes for students with learning and special education needs. Along with other forms of MTSS (including Positive Behavior Intervention and Support, or PBIS), systems like RTI have been implemented widely in schools, and have been recommended for the private Christian school setting as well (Dombrowski and Slater 2021).

Regardless of the specific formulation or target population, the MTSS is typically structured as follows:

- *Tier 1*, which focuses on **prevention**, is composed of general or universal interventions, which are measures put into place to benefit and support all students;

- *Tier 2*, which focuses on **individualized intervention**, comprises targeted strategies to serve students with identified patterns of needs; and

- *Tier 3*, which focuses on **intensive support** or **crisis response**, involves intensive and individualized intervention, typically for students with diagnosed needs and/or those in crisis.

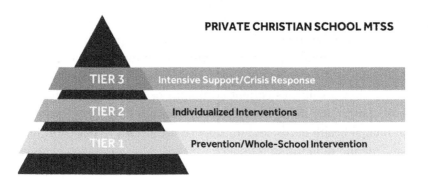

PRIVATE CHRISTIAN SCHOOL MTSS

TIER 3 — Intensive Support/Crisis Response

TIER 2 — Individualized Interventions

TIER 1 — Prevention/Whole-School Intervention

Tier 1 – Prevention/Whole-School Intervention

The focus of Tier 1 is prevention, both individual and schoolwide. This is the tier where concerns are commonly overlooked, yet early intervention can be the most impactful. According to the Child Mind Institute (2016), "early intervention helps to prevent behavioral issues from developing into problems that lead to suspension, expulsion and dropping out. One of the most important components of early intervention of behavioral and emotional health concerns is early identification. School is the ideal place for this." Early intervention prepares students with healthy coping strategies that allow for growth and the development of resilience.

Whole-school intervention efforts that are aimed at prevention include offering student life services, mentoring, awareness programs, psychoeducation resources, support groups, and speakers on topics that address prevalent needs in the school community. Ideally, these programs or groups are evidence-based, are implemented at the start of the school year and continued throughout, and include the whole school as an effort to promote awareness and prevention. If a student attended one of these programs or groups, this should be indicated in their file.

Individual student needs at the level of prevention would mean there is a possibility for distress, or that distress could grow, but the student is not presenting a pattern of frequent or longstanding symptoms or behavior, at high degrees of intensity. Further examples of needs at this level include when a staff person is concerned for a student, but there is limited evidence to support the concern; a student's natural supports are compromised (e.g., family disruption) and/or a student is exposed to multiple stressors; minimal risk is posed by a student's current symptoms or behavior, in terms of both danger and disruption; a student does not have a past history of mental health needs; and/or supports are already in place for the student and monitoring is underway.

Case Study: Tier 1

Anxiety: A student glances at the clock multiple times throughout a class period. He appears to be fidgety and less engaged. There is no previous history of mental health concerns and the student is academically very strong. When the teacher asks if the student is OK, he breaks down in tears and says that there is no way he can do well on the exam. He says he cannot focus during exams because his mind goes blank, his heart races, and he feels as if he can't catch his breath. This makes his fear of failure even worse.

Depression: A student who was previously academically strong and very involved in the theater program has shown a disinterest in school or socializing with friends, including trying out for the school musical. When the point person at the school meets with the student, she reports that recently she has stopped enjoying many things, but she can't identify a reason for how she is feeling. She reports that while she is eating three meals a day, she sometimes experiences a loss of appetite and feels like she's forcing herself to eat; she also reports sleeping more than usual. While the student recently lost her grandmother to cancer, she does not bring that up as a correlation with her current emotional state. The point person confirms that the student is not experiencing suicidal ideation or engaging maladaptive behaviors, but remains concerned about the student's well-being.

Needs in Tier 1 can be addressed by support groups in the school and community, which can educate and encourage skill building (e.g., social skills groups, emotional support groups). Online resources (such as relaxation apps, sleep audios, gratitude journals) are also available that can help mitigate Tier 1 concerns.

Tier 2 – Individualized Interventions

Tier 2 encompasses mental health concerns that have developed into patterns of behavior. This tier represents the problem behaviors that are growing—in frequency and/or duration—in a direction that would become potentially dangerous or disruptive, either to the student or others, if they continue to progress. Tier 2 also engages students that are declining in multiple areas (e.g., both academics and relationships) or withdrawing or self-isolating.

When symptoms or behaviors fall into Tier 2, professional mental health support or treatment is needed. As mentioned in Chapter 7, these professionals are often not employed by the school, and therefore constitute the student's outside support team. Examples of the types of outside professionals who may provide support are listed below:

- **Behavior specialist (ABA):** Typically provided by school district support if there is a mental health or related diagnosis, and is provided as part of a plan for accommodations. The behavior specialist tracks problem behaviors and utilizes specific interventions to extinguish the problem behaviors, by replacing them with appropriate behaviors that are adaptive for students' growth.

- **Mobile Therapists:** Provided by most school districts as a support service that provides therapy in the home, community, or the school. This therapy is typically aligned with a behaviorist approach, but is geared toward helping the child sort through difficult emotions or family dynamics.

- **Independent Case Management:** Case managers are professionals trained to assist in coordinating services to support mental health in the community.

- **Marriage and Family Therapist (LMFT):** An individual who is trained to work specifically with the family or relational systems.

- **Licensed Professional Counselor (LPC or LMHC)**: Counselors who are trained in specific therapeutic modalities.

- **Licensed Clinical Social Worker (LCSW)**: Social workers trained in the system of supports, case management, and counseling.

- **Psychologist**: Doctoral-level therapists trained for assessment, evaluation to diagnose, and counseling.

- **Psychiatrists**: Medical doctors trained to evaluate, diagnose, and prescribe medication.

- **Nurse Practitioners**: Work with psychiatrists to manage medications and can prescribe medication with the oversight of a psychiatrist.

- **Intensive Outpatient Programs**: Therapeutic support groups for more intensive services to support mental health concerns, which provide daily or every-other-day support to assess mental health needs and intervene with positive coping skills, typically two to three hours after school. Appropriate referrals to these programs would be students experiencing extreme levels of emotional, mental, or social distress without medical necessity for hospitalization; these students are also able to manage school but need daily therapeutic support to reinforce healthy coping.

- **Specialized Therapeutic Services**: A range of therapists can provide targeted therapy and treatment in areas like eating disorders, autism services, and so forth.

In addition to the outside support team, a student support plan (discussed later in this chapter) is necessary. The support plan should have interventions that are measurable and include SMART goals (Specific, Measurable, Attainable, Realistic, and Time Limited), along with regular documentation and evaluation that are used to guide decisions. The support plan should accurately represent the support that the school is able to provide, with the coordination of outside mental health professionals who compose the student's external support team.

Anxiety: A student has a behavioral pattern and a history of panic. The panic seems to come on strong in afternoon classes, and lasts for up to ten minutes. The number of days the student experiences panic has been increasing in intensity and frequency the past week. The student manages it by requesting to go to the bathroom, where she breathes into a bag that she carries. After a few minutes, the student returns to the classroom appearing exhausted. There has been no formal treatment or history of intervention. The panic is reducing the student's ability to focus in class and her academic performance has been negatively affected.

Depression: A student reaches out to the school counselor to make an appointment to talk. The student reports that recently his sense of hopelessness has been increasing. He is withdrawn socially and has limited supports. The student is involved in sports, but recently did not make the varsity team during tryouts. Since then, the student has requested to go home during the day, several times a week. His grades are plummeting, and he has recently begun neglecting his physical appearance, often wearing the same clothing for multiple days. He expresses a wish to "disappear," but has no thoughts of suicide, no intent to self-harm, no plan, and no access to means to hurt himself.

Tier 3 - Intensive Support/Crisis Response

Tier 3 problems are those symptoms or behaviors that have reached a point where they are significantly *dangerous* or *disruptive*, either to the student or to others. Tier 3 is Crisis Response where the response must be immediate, by a team that has been trained and has assigned roles with clear duties in crisis situations. Behaviors or symptoms must be handled immediately, with a prescribed protocol. [Chapter 9 provides in-depth look at crisis intervention in the school setting.] When symptoms or behaviors fall into Tier 3, immediate professional mental health support or treatment is needed.

Case Study: Tier 3

Anxiety: A student presents with an episode of panic that is intense and prolonged. The student has no coping skills in place to manage the episode, which disrupts the class period when the student begins shaking and crying uncontrollably. The student is brought to the nurse's office as a safe space, but the episode continues to escalate until the student appears to be having a seizure. The anxiety attack appears to have triggered a preexisting health condition and the student is in physical danger. In accordance with the school's crisis procedures, the school nurse calls 911 and activates the school's crisis response team.

Depression: A student writes in a text to a friend that she has been cutting recently to numb the pain, but that this week she has been hoping that she might go too far. The friend shows the text to the teacher, who reports the student to the point person. The point person meets with the student right away, who reports that there is an extreme sense of hopelessness due to a recent relationship break up. The student has been cutting for the past three months to manage the pain, has been isolating, and reports a wish to be dead. She also reports access to cutting devices hidden throughout her house, and shares that she constantly plays out in her mind a plan to cut and then immerse herself in the bathtub, with the hopes of bleeding out and ending it all. Given that there is suicidal ideation, a plan, a history, and access to means, the school's crisis intervention team is activated to get immediate professional evaluation and care for this student.

Examples of the types of outside professionals who may intervene in a crisis situation are listed below:

- **Mobile Crisis Teams**: Two or three trained professionals who can come to the school, evaluate emergency situations, and coordinate care for the student and the family.

- **Hospital ER**: A hospital provides 24/7 evaluation and medical support. If a student is in imminent danger or reports suicidal ideation, an evaluation and recommendations from a medical doctor would be required immediately. A hospital also provides a safe space for the individual, if needed, until other services can be coordinated. The school is only required to get the individual to the hospital, which will coordinate care upon arrival—up to and possibly including hospitalization, if deemed necessary after evaluation.

- **Partial Hospitalization Programs (PHP)**: Partial hospitalization programs provide a safe, therapeutic space daily for up to six hours. They are a step down from hospitalization or provide intervention for social, emotional, or mental challenges that impede daily functioning or safety concerns. Students may be referred to these programs following a level of care evaluation by a mental health professional. In addition to daily medication management and therapeutic skills training, partial programs have an educational component; students bring schoolwork and there is typically an educational liaison who works with the school to coordinate academics. The idea of these programs is to gradually reduce supports and reincorporate students back into school. While mental health professionals in these programs will guide the process of discharge and return to school, the school needs to be ready with questions on interventions, plans, and support services to put into place after the PHP.

Putting the MTSS into Practice

Having a system of support in place to manage needs contributes to a positive culture around mental health, where student challenges can be seen as points of growth and resilience rather than symptoms of dysfunction. Appropriate support and involvement of mental health professionals is necessary so that needs are addressed optimally and risk is reduced, but as importantly, with the appropriate supports in place, students should gradually need less support and move towards greater independence. The remainder of this chapter will address the key elements necessary for putting the MTSS into practice: *staffing; referral forms; initial assessment; follow-up procedures; initial team meeting; student support plans; and monitoring and reassessment.*

Staffing the MTSS

As discussed in Chapter 7, not all Christian schools have mental health professionals or school counselors on staff. This does not preclude the development of an MTSS for mental health needs; in fact, it makes the MTSS all the more important. By assessing students' needs by tier, school staff can easily discern when collaboration with local mental health professionals to consult, evaluate, and intervene with students is needed. Again, clear procedures and policies, and creating a system of care with outside professionals, is key. Within the school, an administrative lead—or point person—and a backup (in case the point person is unavailable) should be identified and tasked with the responsibilities of conducting initial screening, assignment to tiers, collaboration with support teams inside and outside of the school, and evaluating the success of support and interventions.

Individuals serving in the role of point person should have some basic training (often through continuing education) in the areas of mental health assessment, recognizing signs of distress, and implementation of interventions. Competencies of the point person should include the ability to build rapport with students and families, leading a team of staff, and the ability to de-escalate and remain calm in stressful situations.

Referral Forms

How does the school know that students are in need of mental health-related assessment and support? The answer is that a referral strategy needs to be in place, by which students are brought to the attention of the point person. If there is a crisis, then the school's crisis response team is activated immediately, but if it is an apparent Tier 1 or Tier 2 concern, then a *referral form* is the appropriate mechanism for alerting the point person. This form can be filled out by a student, a teacher, an administrator, other school staff person (e.g., coach), or potentially a parent. The referral form should request the following types of information:

- Student's name, grade, and homeroom teacher

- Referring individual's name and contact information

- Date of referral

- Description of presenting problem, to include how long, how often, and how intense

- Description of what has been tried to address the problem, along with an assessment of what has worked and what has not worked

- Any additional pertinent information that is known, such as family context, social context, or cultural considerations

In addition to this section for the referring individual to complete, there should be an administrative section at the bottom or back of each form. This should provide space to note the following:

- Date and time scheduled for the point person's initial session with the student

- Tier assignment

- Intervention(s) implemented

- Time frame for check in (e.g., weekly, twice a week, etc.)
- Family communication plan
- Communication with referring party (follow-up)

The referral form is important because it allows students or teachers to understand there is a process for presenting problems and it streamlines communication in one direction. It also alleviates side conversations, or multiple long conversations, by providing just the information needed for the point person to meet directly with the student and begin addressing the concern. It also provides a starting point for documentation by noting the exact time/date that the issue was presented. [Chapter 7 provides guidance for creating and storing student files.] If there are concerns in the future, the referral form provides a reference point for how the initial presentation of behavior or symptoms was handled. And finally, it enables the point person, and the student support team, to create and document strategies based on the level of need presented.

Initial Assessment

For mental health practitioners, the first step in assessing the severity of a presenting problem is to conduct what's called a *level of care assessment*. This assessment is used by practitioners to measure the severity of symptoms and determine the supports that need to be put in place for those symptoms to decrease, the client's safety to be preserved, and progress to be measured. In every hospital and mental health treatment facility, there is a mental health professional whose job it is to do this assessment. If a school has a licensed mental health professional on staff, that individual can likewise administer the assessment. It is important to note that while educators like principals and deans do have valuable positions on a support team, they should not lead mental health or school psychological services unless they are licensed mental health professionals as well.

This does not, however, preclude educators at the school from conducting a general assessment of the severity of the presenting problem, and identifying the tier in which the presenting problem falls. In such a scenario (and as with the student who is about to show up at the principal's office in our opening example for this chapter), the purpose of an assessment administered by the school is triage, not treatment. A checklist can be used by the school point person to assess the level of severity. Again, it is important for the point person to have basic training in the areas of mental health assessment, recognizing signs of distress, and implementation of interventions, which will enable the point person to assign student needs to the appropriate tier of the MTSS.

Case Study:

A counselor had been hired to work at a Christian school in student support. The counselor was given a list of names of children K-12 that had behavioral, social, or emotional, or learning challenges. Students were divided into elementary and high school and then listed alphabetically. In some cases, just the student's name was listed; in others, one or two bullet points listed the student's symptoms and/ or actions the school had taken in the past.

During a monthly Student Support Team meeting, each child on the list was discussed on a case-by-case basis. This method was intended to bring students to the attention of all administrators and student support staff. However, there were up to forty students on the list, and it was difficult to get to each one. The team would go down the list from the top, but the list was not organized by the priority of the need. If time ran out and a student's name was on the bottom of the list, it was likely they would not be covered in that month's discussion. The counselor also noted that after the meeting, it took a lot of time to discuss each case with any team members who had been absent, both to collect any additional information they may have and fill them in on the details.

The counselor, having come out of a job in a behavioral health system, noted that though there were a lot of important pieces created by the school to acknowledge and support student needs, the school was lacking a system for identifying, assessing, prioritizing, and tracking student needs. The counselor noted that this was putting students at risk and left the school with enormous vulnerabilities.

After that first meeting, the counselor met with the dean of students and proposed the implementation of an MTSS that organized student mental health needs into three tiers, based on severity of the concerns—thereby creating a very clear road map of how concerns could be categorized, discussed properly, and addressed. The new system would provide a common language for procedures and protocols for each presenting problem. Once in place, the system would provide the backbone for an effective, coordinated approach to handling mental health needs at the school, including a structure for the Student Support Team meeting.

Follow-Up Procedures

As discussed in Chapter 7, a specific protocol, with detailed procedures for handling mental health needs, should be developed by the school. This protocol is then followed after the initial assessment. Having this prepared ahead of time alleviates time it takes to figure out how to handle presenting problems "in the moment" and ensures that student care and documentation are appropriate.

The school's follow-up protocol and procedures should be developed by the school's Student Support Team, in consultation with mental health professionals who understand the school's resources and context. While it is important to note that schools will have varying interventions as options based on the resources available at the school (including whether there are mental health professionals on staff), the table on the next page is offered as a sample of follow-up procedures.

Tier	Procedures/Action Steps
Tier 1: **Prevention**	1. Referral form filled out by student or the referring party. 2. Point person schedules session with the student to check in and conduct initial assessment of presenting problem. 3. Point person documents assessment, steps to be taken, and follow up plans, and creates secure student file if one does not yet exist. 4. Point person contacts parents or guardians for follow-up. 5. Point person contacts referring party for follow-up. 6. Point person implements school support for the next month (depending on the need presented, school support might be academic tutoring, mentoring, etc.). 7. Point person schedules follow-up sessions with the student to track the presenting problem and monitor progress. 8. Point person provides education and resources for student to access if the need escalates. 9. Point person adds student name to the Student Support Team caseload, under Tier 1.

Tier	Procedures/Action Steps
Tier 2: **Individualized Intervention**	1. Referral form filled out by student or the referring party. 2. Point person schedules session with the student to check in and conduct initial assessment of presenting problem. 3. Point person documents assessment, steps to be taken, and follow-up plans, and creates secure student file if one does not yet exist. 4. Point person arranges a team meeting (with student present, if age appropriate—typically over the age of 14), parents or guardians, referring party (if appropriate), and other supports (learning, school nurse, student support staff). 5. Referrals to outside providers made and release forms signed by parents or guardians for school to communicate with providers (see the sample provided in the Resources section). 6. Student support plan (discussed later in this chapter) or behavior contract created with SMART goals, which is signed by parents or guardians, student (if age appropriate), and support team. 7. Follow-up meeting scheduled to assess progress and update student support plan. 8. Point person adds student name to the Student Support Team caseload, under Tier 2. 9. Ongoing monitoring to assess evidence of progress, to determine either to proceed with the intervention strategy, make changes to the plan, or decide whether the school has sufficient resources to continue to support the student.

Tier	Procedures/Action Steps
Tier 3: **Intensive Intervention/ Crisis Response**	1. Crisis team is activated, with each member of the team performing their assigned duties (see Chapter 9, which details crisis response in a school setting). 2. Person physically with the student escorts him/her to a safe space for de-escalation procedures. 3. Emergency services contacted if necessary. 4. Student leaves campus safely for advanced care. 5. Point person documents the situation, steps that were taken, and follow-up plans, and creates secure student file if one does not yet exist. 6. Team meeting is arranged to outline terms for return. 7. Letter is written to parents/guardians outlining terms of return, along with request for release forms for school to speak with outside providers (see the sample provided in the Resources section). 8. If/when the student returns, the student is assigned to Tier 2 and a student support plan is put into place, with evaluation of progress scheduled within a set period of time.

Initial Team Meeting

For students with Tier 2 needs, a meeting with parents or guardians and the full student support team will be necessary. Invitations to this first meeting (whether by phone or letter) should be short and to the point; it should be shared with parents or guardians that the meeting will be the time to elaborate on concerns and to answer questions. In addition to parents or guardians, all team members and the student should be at the meeting. In preparation for the initial meeting, the school point person should gather the names and numbers of outside providers that would be relevant for the case, prepare releases to speak with outside providers (see the sample provided in the Resources section), and prepare the student support plan template (see the final section of this chapter). The point person should also ensure the school's documentation and the student case file are up to date.

Initial meetings should begin by noting the student's strengths. This is imperative and sets the tone for the family, student, and school staff, that these meetings are not just to talk about problems, but also to recognize how the problems are impeding student's growth. After the team has shared strengths, a list can be gathered of existing supports that the family or student has already. This might be mental health providers, church and community support, and so forth. If the child has any medical or psychological conditions that are diagnosed, this should be noted as well. Finally, while certainly not all mental health concerns in schools involve abuse or neglect, school staff need to be aware of the possibility that either may be uncovered in meetings (each state has a phone number that mandated reporters are required to call to report child abuse or neglect; school staff should be trained as mandated reporters in accordance with state law, as well as required by the school's insurance carrier).

Next, the team should identify and name the problem behaviors or emotional concerns. It is important to start with those concerns that are most disruptive or pose the most potential danger, if they continue. After the concerning behavior is noted as specifically as possible (for example, "the student regularly pushes other students at recess, and seems to target male students who are younger"), a SMART goal should be formulated to address the concern (Specific, Measurable, Attainable, Realistic, and Time Limited). Goals that are vague create challenges and ambiguity. The "deliverables" of this initial meeting include a student support plan (detailed in the next section) as well as release forms signed by the parents/guardians and student so that the school can communicate with outside providers (see the sample provided in the Resources section). These forms adhere to confidentiality policy and allow communication about the case; if they are not signed, the provider cannot legally speak with school staff about confidential information.

Student Support Plans

Student support plans are created by the whole team, including the student and parents/guardians, and set clear goals for progress, outline objectives for meeting the goals, and specify a time frame so that the effectiveness of interventions can be determined. Support plans can be applied to behavioral, emotional, social, general health, or academic concerns, and provide clear documentation that not only aids the student but also protects the school as well. It is important to note that this plan is not an Individualized Education Plan (IEP) or a Behavior Plan developed by an ABA therapist; rather, it is a school-generated plan that provides a way of documenting and tracking a strategy, and clarifying roles and responsibilities of providers, parents, the student, and the school to meet agreed-upon goals.

As mentioned earlier, the support plan should have interventions that are measurable and include SMART goals (Specific, Measurable, Attainable, Realistic, and Time Limited), along with regular documentation and evaluation that are used to guide decisions. The support plan should accurately represent the support that the school is able to provide, with the coordination of outside mental health professionals who compose the student's external support team. The plan should specify each of the responsibilities of the family, the student, the school, and the providers to reach the articulated goals (see the Resources section for a sample support plan).

A time frame should be set to reassess progress (the time frame should be shorter if the student's behaviors are more dangerous or disruptive). Finally, the student support plan should be signed and dated by the parents or guardians, the student (if age appropriate), and the members of the Student Support Team at the school. With parent/guardian permission (and student permission, if age appropriate), the plan can be copied and be given to each member of the team.

Monitoring and Reassessment

A follow-up meeting should be scheduled at the end of the first meeting. Ideally, the whole team would be present in the second meeting. The follow-up meeting should allow for sufficient time to implement the agreed upon interventions, but close to the first meeting enough to ensure that concerns that do not resolve or get worse can be addressed quickly (in general, the more dangerous or disruptive the behavior, the shorter the amount of time before follow-up meetings).

In advance of follow-up meetings, it is important to have ongoing monitoring occurring, to collect on the effectiveness of the agreed-upon interventions. If a mental health professional is involved in the case, then they should be the one collecting data, as they will have specific measures and will guide that process. For example, school districts will often provide ABA therapists to facilitate procedures for more difficult behaviors; these providers are required to collect data on progress, and if parents/guardians sign the release form for the school, then access to this data and intervention strategy can be given to the school to track progress. The school point person should also plan to communicate with outside providers (e.g., licensed counselors, psychiatrists prescribing medication, etc.) in advance of follow-up meetings, to gauge progress outside of the school. The individual who completed the referral form (e.g., the homeroom teacher, coach, or other school staff person) should also complete an observation form to track the frequency, duration, and intensity of the concern or behavior since the initial meeting.

All of this data will help to inform decisions regarding the appropriate level of support (e.g., continue, increase, decrease), which should be made at the reassessment meeting. The reassessment meeting must include a parent or guardian, the school point person, and any other members of the team who can attend, including the student. The format of this meeting should be similar to that of the initial meeting: recognize strengths and areas of growth from the last meeting; note progress toward the SMART goals, including what interventions helped and did not help; and make a determination whether to adjust the current student support plan, continue as written, or assess if the school is able to adequately meet the student's needs. If the latter, the school should have options thought through ahead of time for other placements that may better fit the student to promote optimal growth.

The hope and prayer is always that, with the appropriate supports in place, students should gradually need less support and move towards greater independence. Through continual monitoring and reassessment, students' trajectory toward greater wholeness and well-being can be mapped, adjusted, and encouraged by the school and those supporting students in that journey.

Crisis Intervention in Christian Schools
Jon Widmier, *Denver Seminary*

The discussion about crisis intervention in schools has never been more relevant or formidable. Suicide among youth aged 10-24 years old has grown 57.4 percent from 2007 to 2018, while during this same time frame, 42 out of 50 states saw suicide rates increase significantly (Curtin 2020). Meanwhile, the Surgeon General of the United States has declared a "national youth mental health crisis" in our nation (U.S. Department of Health & Human Services 2021). Schools are seeing dramatic increases in the social emotional needs of students, and the increase in suicidal ideation is also growing: "Schools oftentimes find themselves at the center of these (suicide rates) increases, for the sheer purpose of that is where students 18 and younger spend the majority of their time" (Mueller et al. 2021).

Ensuring that schools have a proper mental health safety net is a necessity. Such a comprehensive approach should include support at the prevention, intervention, and postvention levels (Joshi et al. 2017). A suicide risk assessment or suicide screener takes place at the intervention level. However, it is important to note that true suicide prevention begins long before intervention and may not include only lists of warning signs, risk factors, or awareness, but rather aspects of connectedness, belonging, and a sense of how to deal with difficult situations (LoMurray et al. 2021). In addition to prevention and postvention work, suicide intervention is quite possibly the most important need to be considered in a comprehensive approach, yet also holds the most complexity. While this chapter addresses suicide intervention primarily, many of the principles can also apply to many other crisis situations that present in the school setting.

Who Can Intervene?

The issue of school counselors conducting risk assessments is one of the more talked about tensions in the work of school counseling. During the summer of 2021, the American School Counselor Association (ASCA) made a firm statement about what a counselor's role should be regarding assessing the suicidal risk of students, stating school counselors should not be a part of suicide risk assessments (Stone 2021). Behind ASCA's reluctance to adopt the use of assessments is a well-founded belief that school counselors are not trained to provide formal assessment or significant intervention for a suicidal student; even definitionally, "Suicide assessment usually refers to a more comprehensive evaluation done by a clinician to confirm suspected suicide risk, estimate the immediate danger to the patient, and decide on a course of treatment" (National Action Alliance 2012). Although school counselors can be licensed professional counselors, they are typically not therapists in a clinical setting when working at a school. They also share none of the protections that therapists have with client privileges and confidentiality.

ASCA's article on suicide assessments by school counselors is a well-thought-out ideology that identifies many perils for school counselors. Unfortunately, this belief system could be misconstrued to imply that it is not the work of a school counselor to provide support to students who are suicidal or at risk of self-harm, or that counselors should be more concerned about liability than supporting and serving students. If school counselors are not the right people to help support students, then who is left? Teachers are already overburdened attempting to meet learning needs and administrators are dealing with a range of issues including discipline incidents. Community partners and agencies are overwhelmed by the increasing mental health needs, the lack of crisis services, and the difficulty of finding a therapist who is accepting patients. It is the work of school counselors to bridge these gaps, and part of the way that they can do that is by being an integral part of a much larger system of support for students.[1]

Suicide intervention or gatekeeper training is essential to creating a safety net for students. A strong recommendation for suicide intervention training would be to utilize one of many evidence-based programs, such as Living Works ASIST training[2] or the QPR Institute's Question, Persuade, Refer training.[3] Such training provides counselors with education in recognizing warning signs, asking the important question of whether a student is suicidal, and helping connect them to safety and support resources. An important distinction made in all of these gatekeeper training programs is that school counselors are seen as connectors, and people that help provide safety for the time being until the student can be connected to the proper mental health resource.

The Intervention Process

Suicide intervention gatekeeper training as a stand-alone practice is not enough, however. Schools should utilize a protocol for an intervention that provides guidance and structured judgment for counselors to help guide them into the next steps. Otherwise, the intervention process defaults to the subjective judgment of the individuals intervening with the student. In developing their mental health protocols—including those related to crisis intervention—schools should consult with licensed mental health professionals, connect with area resources, and follow research-based practices. [The importance of these protocols and the development process was described in the preceding chapter.]

---

[1] It should be noted that some faith-based private schools may not have a licensed school counselor on staff. In such situations, the discussion in this chapter can be applied to other student support staff who would be called upon to intervene in mental health crisis situations.

[2] https://www.livingworks.net

[3] https://qprinstitute.com

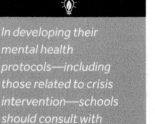

In developing their mental health protocols—including those related to crisis intervention—schools should consult with licensed mental health professionals, connect with area resources, and follow research-based practices.

The ideal scenario for crisis intervention is that counselors conduct a suicide intervention utilizing gatekeeper training, while following a screening tool (for example, using the skills learned in an ASIST training, paired with school crisis protocols, and a tool to help provide structured judgement like the Columbia Suicide Severity Rating Scale Screener). While there is no universal agreement on the definition or utility of either suicide screening or assessment, "most experts agree that a process by which people at risk for suicide can be identified and referred to treatment is an essential component of a comprehensive suicide prevention program" (Suicide Prevention Resource Center 2014). Utilizing a screening tool helps to ensure specific questions are asked of students to help determine a level of concern for the student.

There are many effective tools and resources available to schools that can help, yet schools must be discerning as to what they incorporate. Finding an assessment that is validated and not proprietary is essential for liability purposes. Two recommendations to consider would be the Columbia Suicide Severity Rating Scale (C-SSRS), and the Collaborative Assessment and Management of Suicidality (CAMS). Incorporating these validated frameworks can help counselors justify their decision-making, follow protocols, and provide reasonable care for the student in need. Validated tools are a must; while their effectiveness can be called into question (American School Counselor Association 2021), it is still better to use a tool that has a research basis and outcomes that state objective criteria for when behaviors become more concerning. There is great danger in using tools that are self-developed that do not show research-based evidence with the population being assessed, as well as not having the resources necessary to implement these tools effectively.

A validated screening tool that can be combined with a full assessment, conducted by an external professional or agency, helps a school counselor come to an evidenced-based judgment in an intervention situation. In cases of immediate danger to the individual student or another person, the school protocol should include keeping the student safe while emergency services are called. If emergency services are deemed not necessary, counselors would then refer the student to an agency or partner to follow up with a more in-depth clinical assessment. Some school communities do not have access to or relationships with local mental health agencies. Unfortunately, this tends to be more commonplace in rural or lower socioeconomic areas, as well as among private schools. While a faith community can help provide resources in the form of people to listen and provide mentorship, these individuals cannot be viewed as a replacement for professional therapy as a crisis intervention. Finding national resources, utilizing telehealth, and creating partnerships with therapists are beginning steps to help address this gap.

Unfortunately screening tools are not fail-safe and may still leave school counselors with many issues to address. The true fear is that an individual may take their life when it could have been prevented. While liability is not the proper motivation behind conducting an intervention, it is an unavoidable factor. The liability that surrounds screening or assessment lies with the school and school counselor, as it falls to them to provide reasonable care of the student and to notify parents or guardians. By having mental health staff participate in gatekeeper training and having a

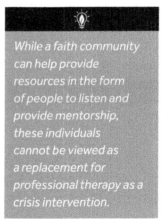

While a faith community can help provide resources in the form of people to listen and provide mentorship, these individuals cannot be viewed as a replacement for professional therapy as a crisis intervention.

protocol and screening tool to ensure proper steps are taken, schools and school counselors can minimize their liability while caring for students and families. Enacting these steps, along with the notification of parents or guardians throughout this process, provides counselors with the protection of following reasonable, and documented, steps to ensure the safety and care of their students.

Involving Parents and Guardians

In all instances, the counselor needs to communicate with parents or guardians that a conversation took place, why it took place, and review how the student answered the questions they were asked. Using a validated tool enables the counselor to convey the outcomes more clearly to parents or guardians and garner more support for the student. Parents and guardians would then be given resources including warning signs, risk factors, and a list of phone numbers to local or national mental health agencies and hotlines, and/or local hospitals. Most importantly, the school counselor ensures the student and their parents or guardians are being connected to a mental health safety net. While this does not guarantee safety, it does remove some level of subjectivity from the evaluation of actual risk.

One key aspect of liability is how risk-level is communicated from counselors to parents and guardians. Even using a validated tool leaves a counselor at risk of concluding a student is "at low risk for suicide" when a counselor simply has no way to guarantee or validate

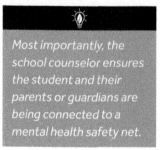

Most importantly, the school counselor ensures the student and their parents or guardians are being connected to a mental health safety net.

that statement. A student could be lying to the counselor, or a counselor may misread the situation. It can be impossible for a school counselor to recognize every instance of suicidal thinking if a student does not want anyone to know; many students are adept at hiding their emotions or may not have a relationship with their counselor where they feel comfortable disclosing their thoughts. There are simply too many variables that could go wrong to assign a "low" level of risk or concern. It is much wiser for the counselor to simply recite the questions asked to the student and their response back to the parents or guardians, and then allow for all concerned to evaluate the student's current safety. For example, a school counselor could call a parent and say, "When asked if your child has thoughts about suicide, they responded 'no.'" By walking through these questions and the student's answers with the parents or guardians, a school counselor lets them know exactly the information that the school knows.

It should also be noted there are many different points where conflict can arise when conveying one's concerns about students to their parents or guardians. For example, parents or guardians may not believe the school counselor and minimize the student's feelings. Minimizing is dangerous not only because this can create a barrier to the student getting support, but also because the underlying message to the student is that they are not being taken seriously. There is then a real danger of a student taking more drastic steps in order to be taken seriously. No situation causes more concern for a counselor than when there is a high level of safety concern for a student which is not met with the same level of concern by their parents or guardians.

A counselor has few desirable options at this point. It is always advisable to be as honest and straightforward as possible. Parents and guardians should always be given the benefit of the doubt that they will do the right thing for their children, yet a school counselor should always document what steps and recommendations they made to the parent or guardian to help ensure student safety. If the parent or guardian has a history of not following through with expectations, then a counselor could potentially do one of any of the following three things:

- First, they could call the Department of Human Services and report the parent or guardian for neglect. Making this phone call could potentially spur action against the parent or guardian or provide resources for the student. It could also severely damage the relationship with the parent or guardian and prevent future work for the student from being accomplished.

- Second, a school can have law enforcement or an ambulance transport the student to an emergency room or mental health facility for an evaluation. As mentioned earlier, this action might be necessary if the student is acutely suicidal or actively attempting suicide at school. If the student is neither, however, this could financially impact the parents or guardians. And if the family must pay for unwarranted ambulance or emergency services, it could compound the student's feelings of being a burden to the family.

- Finally, the simplest and most relationally difficult option would be to address concerns about the parent or guardian directly with them, in an honest and straightforward manner. While difficult, a direct conversation allows a school to let the parents or guardians know the level of, and cause for, concern, and that the counselor and the family only have one chance and do not want to be wrong. The follow-through on a conversation of this nature is extremely important. A school cannot have these conversations and then not continue to speak to the parents about what barriers they could be facing, and what help they might need to take the recommended or required actions.

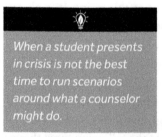

When a student presents in crisis is not the best time to run scenarios around what a counselor might do.

All of these scenarios and options should be planned for in the school's protocols, which again, should be developed in conjunction with licensed mental health professionals and connect to both area resources and research-based practices. When a student presents in crisis is not the best time to run scenarios around what a counselor might do if a parent or guardian denies the seriousness of the situation, or refuses to follow through on the request for a clinical assessment to be performed by a licensed professional. Having protocols in place for handling various student and parent or guardian responses is crucial. To reiterate, when developed with professional consultation, these protocols can provide counselors with the protection of following reasonable, and documented, steps to ensure the safety and care of their students.

Postvention

A crisis situation does not end after the point of intervention. Postvention, or follow-up, is crucial. An effective way to follow through after an assessment or screening of a suicidal student is to hold follow-up meetings. [See Chapter 8 for further discussion of follow-up meetings, as part of systematizing support for students.] For students with whom there are lower levels of concern, these meetings can be done on an individual basis. For students with a more significant level of concern, the development of a safety plan—which highlights their coping skills and resources of people to talk to—is essential. A safety plan should not be punitive in nature, but

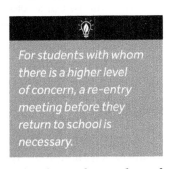

For students with whom there is a higher level of concern, a re-entry meeting before they return to school is necessary.

there may be punitive aspects. For example, if a student indicated a plan to self-injure at school, they may lose the use of a hall pass, or must use a restroom in the main office for supervision purposes.

For students with whom there is a higher level of concern, a re-entry meeting before they return to school is necessary. Administrators, parents, trusted adults, and any outside mental health partners who have a relationship should be in attendance. Discussion of steps taken, treatment plans, and the student's safety net are vital. Along with discussing any issues, or stressors, the school can help with (e.g., homework, passing periods, bullying), re-entry meetings are also a great place to discuss any concerns or problems that parents or guardians might be experiencing such as access to care or issues with school staff. Discussion of these issues allows the school to partner with the family towards a positive result. The more school staff can talk about these barriers, the more it demystifies mental health and the stigma or label that a student or family might feel because of an assessment or screening process.

Finally, while no school or counselor would ever want to plan for it, in the event that a suicide has taken place, strong postvention work is critical. The trauma of a suicide affects both students and educators alike and schools should create a plan to support both groups with mental health resources, which can often be provided by community agencies or mental health professionals who are properly trained. Such support is not just reactive, but also preventative in nature, as it reduces the risk of suicide contagion—or increases in suicides or suicidal behaviors, due to exposure to a suicide—in a community (American Foundation of Suicide Prevention and Suicide Prevention Resource Center 2018).

Conclusion

Regardless of the specific language one uses in describing assessments or screening tools, levels of concern, or risk, helping students in crisis is the heart of a counselor's work. The work is high stakes, stressful, and unfortunately, growing. More is being asked of schools in general, and as a result, more is being asked of school counselors. It is important to always work with empathy and compassion. A school counselor may have to make more than one intervention in the course of a week, or even a day, but every person they come into contact with must feel like their situation is the only one that matters.

Hopefully, the steps and resources described in this chapter will assist schools as they help as many people as possible. In the midst of discussions of risk and liability, it is essential to remember that ultimately, our greatest call and concern is for the student. Similar to the call of Queen Esther, who placed herself at risk for the sake of her people, we have a choice to step into that risk for the sake of our students. As Esther is asked in Scripture, "And who knows but that you have come to your...position for such a time as this?" (Esther 4:14, NIV).

Resources for Mental Health & Well-Being in Christian Schools

We conclude this monograph with a selection of helpful resources and references that are intended to support mental health and well-being in Christian schools. On the following pages readers will find:

1. **Sample Release Form**—to be signed by parents/guardians (and the student, when applicable) so that the school has permission to speak with outside mental health professionals and providers regarding the student's case and care.
2. **Sample Student Support Plan**—to be developed by the Student Support Team in consultation with the student, parents/guardians, and input from outside mental health professionals and providers (as applicable).

In addition, the monograph authors recommend the following resources for further exploration and study:

The American School Counselor Association (ACSA) Resources:

- Model: https://www.schoolcounselor.org/school-counselors-members/asca-national-model
- Free Toolkits: https://www.schoolcounselor.org/Publications-Research/Publications/Free-ASCA-Resources

Issue-Specific Resources on:

- Bullying: https://www.stopbullying.gov/
- Grief and Loss: https://www.nasponline.org/resources-and-publications/resources-and-podcasts/school-safety-and-crisis/mental-health-resources/addressing-grief
- Drug Use/Abuse: https://teens.drugabuse.gov/
- Trauma-Informed Education: Greene, R. W. 2009. *Lost at school: Why our kids with behavioral challenges are falling through the cracks and how we can help them.* Simon and Schuster.

Mental Health Programs and Assessment Resources:

- Evidenced-based Social Emotional Education programs: https://casel.org/
- Multi-Tiered System of Supports (MTSS): https://www.pbisrewards.com/blog/what-is-mtss/
- Sources of Strength: https://sourcesofstrength.org/
- Needs Assessment of a School Population: http://www.thehelpful-counselor.com/school-counseling-needs-assessment/
- Suicide Evaluation/Prevention:
  a. https://afsp.org/model-school-policy-on-suicide-prevention
  b. https://qprinstitute.com/
  c. https://cssrs.columbia.edu/

State and Local Resources:

In many cases, state boards of education will produce guidelines for mental health and crisis prevention in schools. These can be helpful resources to review, as can any resources developed by local school districts or local education agencies (LEAs). One example:

- West Virginia Board of Education. 2017. *Addressing mental health in school crisis prevention & response: A resource guide for West Virginia schools.* Available at: https://wvde.us/wp-content/uploads/2018/01/Addressing-Mental-Health-in-School-Crisis-Prevention-Response.pdf.

Resources for Educator Well-Being in Christian Schools

- For school leaders who want to design an employee wellness strategy to support teacher well-being in their school: www.goodhealthforgoodworks.org/acsimodel
- For individual teachers and staff who want to create an attainable and sustainable personal well-being plan for 2022: www.goodhealthforgoodworks.org/acsigoals
- Visit https://rexmiller.com/ for teacher workbooks and related resources

SAMPLE RELEASE FORM

(Insert School Logo/Utilize School Letterhead)

Student Name: _____ **Grade:** _____

I, _____ (student name),

do hereby authorize the provider listed below to

obtain/release (circle) information **to/from** (circle)

_____ (name of school).

PROVIDER NAME	
PRACTICE/AGENCY	
ADDRESS	
PHONE	
EMAIL	

I understand that permission can be revoked at any time, in writing, and will be in effect for:

_____ One year from today's date

_____ Other: _____

_____   _____
Student Signature (if over 14)   Date

_____   _____
Parent/Guardian Signature   Date

_____
Parent/Guardian Name (print)

SAMPLE STUDENT SUPPORT PLAN

(Insert School Logo/Utilize School Letterhead)

Student Name: _____ **Date:** _____

Teacher: _____ **Grade:** _____

Background Information:

Diagnosis (if applicable)	
Medications with dosing (if applicable)	
Current Outside Support Services (for each, provide name, agency/ organization, and contact number)	

Describe the student's **natural supports** (community involvement, activities, family, friends, church):

_____

_____

Describe the student's **strengths**:

_____

_____

_____

Describe the student's **interests/recreational activities**:

_____

_____

_____

Improvement Targets:

Problem Behavior 1:

_____

Description of Problem: (frequency/duration/intensity/setting/time of day):

_____

_____

_____

_____

SMART Goal (include indicators for knowing when goal has been met):

_____

_____

_____

_____

Intervention Strategy:

_____

_____

_____

Supports Needed:

_____

_____

_____

Outline of Responsibilities

Student's Responsibility	
Parent/Guardian Responsibility	
Outside Provider's Responsibility	

School's Responsibility	

Problem Behavior 2:

_____

Description of Problem: (frequency/duration/intensity/setting/ time of day):

_____

_____

_____

_____

SMART Goal (include indicators for knowing when goal has been met):

_____

_____

_____

Intervention Strategy:

_____

_____

_____

Supports Needed:

_____

_____

_____

Outline of Responsibilities

Student's Responsibility	
Parent/Guardian Responsibility	
Outside Provider's Responsibility	

School's Responsibility	

Date of next meeting and anticipated time of goal completion:

_____

Meeting Participants:

By signing this document I am agreeing to the terms outlined in this plan to support _____ (student name) to reach the goals by adhering to the responsibilities determined by the team.

Name: _____

Signature: _____

Date: _____

Name: _____

Signature: _____

Date: _____

Name: _____

Signature: _____

Date: _____

Name: _____

Signature: _____

Date: _____

REFERENCES

Introduction

Ketchen, S., E.G. Lattie, and D. Eisenberg. 2018. "Increased rates of mental health service utilization by U.S. college students: 10-year population-level trends (2007-2017)." *American Psychiatric Association*, 5 November 2018.

Lever, N., E. Mathis, and A. Mayworm. 2019. "School mental health is not just for students: Why teacher and school staff wellness matter." *Report on Emotional and Behavioral Disorders in Youth* 17, no. 1: 6-12.

Miller, R., B. Latham, K. Baird, and M. Kinder. 2020. *WHOLE: What teachers need to help students thrive.* San Francisco: Jossey-Bass.

Swaner, L.E., and M.H. Lee. 2020. *Christian schools and COVID-19: 2020-2021 school year profile.* Colorado Springs, CO: Association of Christian Schools International.

Swaner, L.E., and A. Wolfe. 2021. *Flourishing together: A Christian vision for students, educators, and schools.* Grand Rapids, MI: Wm. B. Eerdmans Publishing.

Will, M. 2021. "Teachers are not OK, even though we need them to be." *EdWeek*, 14 September 2021. Available at: https://www.edweek.org/teaching-learning/teachers-are-not-ok-even-though-we-need-them-to-be/2021/09.

Part I: Philosophy and Research

1. Defining Well-Being in Christian Schools

Centers for Disease Control and Prevention (CDC). 2013. "Mental health surveillance among children—United States, 2005-2011." *CDC Morbidity and Mortality Weekly Report* 62, no. 2.

Crouch, A. 2017. *The tech-wise family: Everyday steps for putting technology in its proper place.* Grand Rapids, MI: Baker Books.

Fottrell, Q. 2017. "There's been a surge in the number of suicide attempts by teenagers and children." *MarketWatch.* Available at: http://www.marketwatch.com/story/the-number-of-children-with-thoughts-of-suicide-and-self-harm-doubled-in-10-years-2017-05-06.

Keyes, C.L.M. 2007. "Promoting and protecting mental health as flourishing: A complementary strategy for improving national mental health." *American Psychologist* 62, no. 2: 95-108.

Meece, J.L. 2002. *Child and adolescent development for educators.* 2nd edition. New York: McGraw-Hill.

Miller, R., B. Latham, and B. Cahill. 2017. *Humanizing the education machine: How to create schools that turn disengaged kids into inspired learners.* San Francisco: Jossey-Bass.

Peterson, J., S. Freedenthal, C. Sheldon, and R. Andersen. 2008. "Nonsuicidal self injury in adolescents." *Psychiatry* 5, no. 11: 20-26.

Racine, N., B.A. McArthur, J.E. Cooke, R. Eirich, J. Zhu, and S. Madigan. 2021. "Global prevalence of depressive and anxiety symptoms in children and adolescents during COVID-19." *Jama Pediatrics* 175, no. 11: 1142-1150.

Stetzer, E. 2013. "Mental illness and the church: New research on mental health from LifeWay Research." *Christianity Today.* Available at: http://www.christianitytoday. com/edstetzer/2013/september/mental-illness-and-church-new-research-on-mental-health-fro.html.

Williams, A. 2017. "Prozac Nation is now the United States of Xanax." *The New York Times.* 10 June 2017. Available at: https://www.nytimes.com/2017/06/10/style/anxiety-is-the-new-depression-xanax.html.

2. Understanding Student Mental Health: Trends, Influences, and Practices

Agnafors, S., C.G. Svedin, L. Oreland, M. Bladh, E. Comasco, and G. Sydsjo. 2017. "A biopsychosocial approach to risk and resilience on behavior in children followed from birth to age 12." *Child Psychiatry Human Development* 48: 584-596.

Ali, M.M., K. West, J.L. Teich, S. Lynch, R. Mutter, and J. Dubenitz. 2019. "Utilization of mental health services in educational setting by adolescents in the United States." *Journal of School Health* 89: 393-401.

ASCA (American School Counselor Association). 2021. *ASCA research report: State of the profession 2020.* Available at: https://www.schoolcounselor.org/getmedia/bb23299b-678d-4bce-8863-cfcb55f7df87/2020-State-of-the-Profession.pdf.

Aranmolate, R., D.R. Bogan, T. Hoard, and A.R. Mawson. 2017. "Suicide risk factors among LGBTQ youth: Review." *JSM Schizophrenia* 2, no. 2: 1011.

Argyriou, E., G. Bakoyannis, and S. Tantaros. 2016. "Parenting styles and trait emotional intelligence in adolescence." *Scandinavian Journal of Psychology* 57, no. 1: 42-49.

Baker, C.N., H. Peele, M. Daniels, M. Saybe, and K.Whalen, S. 2021. "The experience of COVID-19 and its impact on teachers' mental health, coping, and teaching." *School Psychology Review* 50, no. 4: 491-504.

Berryman, C., C.J. Ferguson, and C. Negy. 2018. "Social media use and mental health among youth adults." *Psychiatric Quarterly* 89, no. 2: 307-314.

Black, S.R., M.L. Evans, L. Aaron, D.R. Brabham, and R.M. Kaplan. 2021. "Covariance between parent and child symptoms before and during the COVID-19 pandemic." *Journal of Pediatric Psychology* 46, no. 10: 1182-1194.

Buckner, J.D., M.E. Keough, and N.B. Schmidt. 2007. "Problematic alcohol and cannabis use among young adults: The roles of depression and discomfort and distress tolerance." *Addictive Behaviors* 32, no. 9: 1957–1963.

Castilho, P., S.A. Carvalho, S. Marques, and J. Pinto-Gouveia. 2017. "Self-compassion and emotional intelligence in adolescence: A multigroup mediational study of the impact of shame memories on depressive symptoms." *Journal of Child and Family Studies* 26, no. 3: 759-768.

References

CDC (Centers for Disease Control and Prevention). 2020. *Youth Risk Behavior Survey data summary & trends report 2007-2017.* Available at: https://npin.cdc.gov/publication/youth-risk-behavior-survey-data-summary-trends-report-2007-2017.

Chang, M. 2009. "An appraisal perspective of teacher burnout: Examining the emotional work of teachers." *Educational Psychology Review* 21, no. 3: 193-218.

Cook, C.R., F.G. Miller, A. Fiat, T. Renshaw, M. Frye, G.Joseph, and P. Decano. 2017. "Promoting secondary teachers' well-being and intentions to implement evidence-based practices: Randomized evaluation of the achiever resilience curriculum." *Psychology in the Schools* 54, no. 1: 13-28.

Crowe, A., P. Averett, J.S. Glass, K.P. Dotson-Blake, S.E. Grissom, D.K. Ficken, and J.A. Holmes. 2016. "Mental health stigma: Personal and cultural impacts on attitudes." *Journal of Counselor Practice* 7, no. 2: 97-119.

Cui, M., C.A. Darling, C. Coccia, F.D. Fincham, and R.W. May. 2019. "Indulgent parenting, helicopter parenting, and well-being of parents and emerging adults." *Journal of Child and Family Studies* 28: 860-871.

Cummings, J., M. Bornovalova, T. Ojanen, E. Hunt, L.MacPherson, and C. Lejuez. 2013. "Time Doesn't Change Everything: The longitudinal course of distress tolerance and its relationship with externalizing and internalizing symptoms during early adolescence." *Journal of Abnormal Child Psychology* 41, no. 5: 735-748.

Curtin, S.C. 2020. "State suicide rates among adolescents and young adults aged 10–24: United States, 2000–2018." *National Vital Statistics Report 2020* 69, no. 11: 1-10.

Dweck, C.S. 2006. *Mindset: The new psychology of success.* New York: Random House.

Ekornes, S. 2017. "Teacher stress related to student mental health promotion: The match between perceived demands and competence to help students with mental health problems." *Scandinavian Journal of Educational Research* 61, no. 3: 333-353.

Erikson, E.H. 1968. *Identity: Youth and crisis.* New York: Norton & Co.

Fardouly, J., N.R. Magson, C.J. Johnco, E.L. Oar, and R.M. Rapee. 2018. "Parental control of the time preadolescents spend on social media: Links with preadolescents' social media appearance comparisons and mental health." *Journal of Youth and Adolescence* 47: 1456-1468.

Fingerman, K.L., Y.P. Cheng, E.D. Wesselmann, S. Zarit, F. Furstenberg, and K.S. Birditt. 2012. "Helicopter parents and landing pad kids: Intense parental support of grown children." *Journal of Marriage and Family* 74, no. 4: 880-896.

Firmin, M.W., K.C. Pugh, R.L. Markham, V.A. Sohn, and E.N. Gentry. 2017. "Perspectives regarding motivations for adoption by Christian adoptive parents: A qualitative study." *Journal of Psychology and Theology* 45, no. 1: 58-68.

Fisher, S., J.L. Reynolds, W.W. Hsu, J. Barnes, and K. Tyler. 2014. "Examining multiracial youth in context: Ethnic identity development and mental health outcomes." *Journal of Youth and Adolescence* 43, no. 10: 1688-1699.

Fletcher, K.L., E.E. Pierson, K.L. Speirs Neumeister, and H. Finch. 2019. "Overparenting and perfectionistic concerns predict academic entitlement in young adults." *Journal of Child and Family Studies* 28: 348-357.

Franbutt, J. M., W. Clark, and G. Speach. 2011. "Supporting mental health and wellness among private school students: A survey of Catholic elementary and secondary schools." *Advances in School Mental Health Promotion* 4, no. 3: 29-41.

Freeman, R., D. Miller, and L. Newcomer. 2015. "Integration of academic and behavioral MTSS at the district level using implementation science." *Learning Disabilities: A Contemporary Journal* 13, no. 1: 59-72.

Getz, G.E. 2014. *Applied biological psychology.* New York: Springer Publishing Company.

Greene, R.W. 2009. *Lost at school: Why our kids with behavioral challenges are falling through the cracks and how we can help them.* New York: Simon and Schuster.

Guinta, M.R., and R.M. John. 2018. "Social media and adolescent health." *Pediatric Nursing* 44, no. 4.

Hadijipanayis, A., E. Efstathiou, P. Altorjai, T. Stiris, A. Valiulis, B. Koletzko, and H. Fonseca. 2019. "Social media and children: What is the pediatrician's role?" *European Journal of Pediatrics* 178: 1605-1612.

Hatchel, T., J.R. Polanin, and D.L. Espelage. 2021. "Suicidal thoughts and behaviors among LGBTQ youth: Meta-analyses and a systematic review." *National Archives of Suicide Research* 25, no. 1: 1-37.

Hartley, L.L. 1990. *The neuropsychology of everyday life: Assessment and basic competencies.* Boston, MA: Springer.

Herman, K.C., W.M. Reinke, A.M. Thompson, K.M. Hawley, K. Wallis, M. Stormont, and C. Peters. 2021. "A public health approach to reducing the societal prevalence and burden of youth mental health problems: Introduction to the special issue." *School Psychology Review* 50, no. 1: 8-16.

Hinojosa, R., J. Nguyen, K. Sellers, and H. Elassar. 2019. "Barriers to college success among students that experienced adverse childhood events." *Journal of American College Health* 67, no. 6: 531-540.

Hiser, J., and M. Koenigs. 2018. "The multifaceted role of the ventromedial prefrontal cortex in emotion, decision making, social cognition, and psychopathology." *Biological Psychiatry* 83, no. 8: 638-647.

HRSA (Health Resources and Services Administration). 2021. "National Survey of Children's Health." Available at: https://mchb.hrsa.gov/sites/default/files/mchb/data-research/national-survey-childrens-health-2021-overview-fact-sheet.pdf.

HRSA (Health Resources and Services Administration). 2020. "Adverse Childhood Experiences NSCH data brief." Available at: https://mchb.hrsa.gov/sites/default/files/mchb/data-research/nsch-ace-databrief.pdf.

Ivey-Stephenson, A.Z., Z. Demissie, A.E. Crosby, D.M. Stone, E. Gaylor, N. Wilkins, and R. Lowry. 2020. "Suicidal ideation and behaviors among high school students - Youth Risk Behavior Survey, United States, 2019." *Morbidity and Mortality Weekly Report Supplements* 69, no. 1: 47-55.

Jennings, P.A., and M.T. Greenberg. 2009. "The prosocial classroom: Teacher social and emotional competence in relation to student and classroom outcomes." *Review of Educational Research* 79, no. 1: 491-525.

References

Jia, H., R.J. Guerin, J.P. Barile, A.H. Okun, L. McKnight-Eily, S.J. Blumberg, and R. Njai. 2021. "National and state trends in anxiety and depression severity scores among adults during the COVID-19 pandemic - United States, 2020-2021." *Morbidity and Mortality Weekly Report* 70: 1427-1432.

Johnson, S., C. Cooper, S. Cartwright, I. Donald, P. Taylor, and C. Millet. 2005. "The experience of work-related stress across occupations." *Journal of Managerial Psychology* 20, no. 2: 178-187.

Keen, D., J. Sigafoos, and G. Woodyatt. 2001. "Replacing prelinguistic behaviors with functional communication." *Journal of Autism and Developmental Disorders* 31, no. 4: 385-398.

Keyes, M.A., A. Sharma, I.J. Elkins, W.G. Iacono, and M. McGue. 2008. "The mental health of US adolescents adopted in infancy." *Archives of Pediatrics & Adolescent Medicine* 162, no. 5: 419-425.

Kiesel, L.R., K.N. Piescher, and J.L. Edleson. 2016. "The relationship between child maltreatment, intimate partner violence exposure, and academic performance." *Journal of Public Child Welfare* 10, no. 4: 434-456.

Knapp, M., and G. Wong. 2020. "Economics and mental health: The current scenario." *World Psychiatry* 19, no. 1: 3-14.

LeCloux, M., P. Maramaldi, K.Thomas, and E. Wharff. 2016. "Family support and mental health service use among suicidal adolescents." *Journal of Child and Family Studies* 25: 2567-2606.

Lemberger-Truelove, M.E., K.J. Carbonneau, D.J. Atencio, A.K. Zieher, and A.F. Palacios. 2018. "Self-regulatory growth effects for young children participating in a combined social and emotional learning and mindfulness-based intervention." *Journal of Counseling & Development* 96, no. 3: 289-302.

Lin, C.Y., P. Namdar, M.D. Griffiths, and A.H. Pakpour. 2020. "Mediated roles of generalized trust and perceived social support in the effects of problematic social media use on mental health: A cross-sectional study." *Health Expectations* 24, no. 1: 165-173.

Mahoney, J.L., A.L. Harris, and J.S. Eccles. 2006. "Organized activity participation, positive youth development, and the over-scheduling hypotheses." *Social Policy Report/Society for Research in Child Development* 20, no. 4: 1-31.

Maslach, C., W.B. Schaufeli, and M.P. Leiter. 2001. "Job burnout." *Annual Review of Psychology* 52, no. 1: 397-422.

Mazalin, D., and S.M. Moore. 2004. "Internet use, identity development and social anxiety among young adults." *Behavior Change* 21, no. 2: 90-102.

McCarthy, C.J., R.G. Lambert, E.W. Crowe, and C.J. McCarthy. 2010. "Coping, stress, and job satisfaction as predictors of Advanced Placement statistics teachers' intention to leave the field." *NASSP Bulletin* 94, no. 4: 306-326.

McDaid, D., A. Park, and K. Wahlbeck. 2019. "The economic case for the prevention of mental illness." *Annual Review of Public Health* 40: 373-389.

Meier Thornton, E., B. Miller, K. Hauser, L. Miller, B. Volpone, and A. Wilson. 2021. "Reflections from the research: Commentary on mental well-being in faith-based P-12 schools." Denver, CO: Denver Seminary, unpublished manuscript.

Moffitt, T.E., L. Arseneault, D. Belsky, N. Dickson, R.J. Hancox, H. Harrington, and R. Houts. 2011. "A gradient of childhood self-control predicts health, wealth, and public safety." *Proceedings of the National Academy of Sciences* 108, no. 7: 693-2698.

Nada-Raja, S., D. Morrison, and K. Skegg. 2003. "A population-based study of help-seeking for self-harm in young adults." *Australian and New Zealand Journal of Psychiatry* 37: 600-605.

Nesi, J. 2020. "The impact of social media on youth mental health." *North Carolina Medical Journal* 81, no. 2: 116-121.

Odgers, C.L., and M.R. Jensen. 2020. "Annual research review: Adolescent mental health in the digital age: Facts, fears, and future directions." *Journal of Child Psychology and Psychiatry* 61, no. 3: 336-348.

Osagiede, O., S. Costa, A. Spaulding, J. Rose, K.E. Allen, M. Rose, and E. Apatu. 2018. "Teachers' perceptions of student mental health: The role of school-based mental health services delivery model." *Children & Schools* 40, no. 4: 240–48.

Pinquart, M., and D.C. Gerke. 2019. "Associations of parenting styles with self-esteem in children and adolescents: A meta-analysis." *Journal of Child and Family Studies* 28, no. 8: 2017-2035.

Posner, K., D. Brent, C. Lucas, M. Gould, B. Stanley, G. Brown, and P. Fisher. 2008. *Columbia-Suicide Severity Rating Scale* (C-SSRS). New York: Columbia University Medical Center.

Racine, N., B.A. McArthur, J.E. Cooke, R. Eirich, J. Zhu, and S. Madigan. 2021. "Global prevalence of depressive and anxiety symptoms in children and adolescents during COVID-19." *Jama Pediatrics* 175, no. 11: 1142-1150.

Ramos-Diaz, E., A. Rodriguez-Fernandez, I. Axpe, and M. Ferrara. 2019. "Perceived emotional intelligence and life satisfaction among adolescent students: The mediating role of resilience." *Journal of Happiness Studies* 20, no. 8: 2489-2506.

Raudsepp, L., and K. Kais. 2019. "Longitudinal associations between problematic social media use and depressive symptoms in adolescent girls." *Preventative Medicine Reports* 15, no. 1.

Reinke, W.M., M. Stormont, K.C. Herman, R. Puri, and N. Goel. 2011. "Supporting children's mental health in schools: Teacher perceptions of needs, roles, and barriers." *Psychology Quarterly* 26, no. 1: 1-13.

Riekie, H., J.M. Aldridge, and E. Afari. 2017. "The role of school climate in high school students' mental health and identity formation: A South Australian study." *British Educational Research Journal* 43, no. 1: 95-123.

Rutter, M. 2006. "Implications of resilience concepts for scientific understanding." *Annals of the New York Academy of Sciences* 1094, no. 1: 1-12.

———. 2012. "Resilience as a dynamic concept." *Development and Psychopathology* 24, no. 2: 335-344.

Schiffrin, H.H., H. Godfrey, M. Liss, and M.J. Erchull. 2014. "Intensive parenting: Does it have the desired impact on child outcomes?" *Journal of Child and Family Studies* 24, no. 8: 2322-2331.

Schiffrin, H.H., M.J. Erchull, E. Sendrick, J.C. Yost, V. Power, and E.R. Saldanha. 2019. "The effects of maternal and paternal helicopter parenting on the self-determination and well-being of emerging adults." *Journal of Child and Family Studies* 28: 3346-3359.

Sciaraffa, M.A., P.D. Zeanah, and C.H. Zeanah. 2018. "Understanding and promoting resilience in the context of adverse childhood experiences." *Early Childhood Education Journal* 46, no. 3: 343–53.

Singer, J. B., T.A. Erbacher, and P. Rosen. 2019. "School-based suicide prevention: A framework for evidence-based practice." *School Mental Health* 11, no. 1: 54-71.

Sink, C.A., R. Cleveland, and J. Stern. 2007. "Spiritual formation in Christian school counseling programs." *Journal of Research on Christian Education* 16, no. 1: 35-63.

Shaw, Z.A., and L.R. Starr. 2019. "Intergenerational transmission of emotional dysregulation: The role of authoritarian parenting style and family chronic stress." *Journal of Child and Family Studies* 28, no. 12: 3508-3518.

Smith, M. 2004. "Parental mental health: Disruptions to parenting and outcomes for children." *Child & Family Social Work* 9, no. 1: 3-11.

Sources of Strength. n.d. Available at: https://sourcesofstrength.org/.

Spies Shapiro, L.A., and G. Margolin. 2013. "Growing up wired: Social networking sites and adolescent psychosocial development." *Clinical Child Family Psychology Review* 17, no. 1: 1-18.

Van Hoof, T.J., T.E. Sherwin, R.C. Baggish, P.B. Tacy, and T.P. Meehan. 2004. "Mental health services at selected private schools." *The Journal of School Health* 74, no. 4: 125-129.

Vannucci, A., and C. McCauley Ohannessian. 2019. "Social media use subgroups differentially predict psychosocial well-being during early adolescence." *Journal of Youth and Adolescence* 48, no. 8: 1469-1493.

Verhoeven, M., A.M.G. Poorthuis, and M. Volman. 2019. "The role of school in adolescents' identity development. A Literature Review." *Educational Psychology Review* 31, no. 1: 35-63.

Walton, G.E., and D.R. Hibbard. 2019. "Exploring adults' emotional intelligence and knowledge of young children's social-emotional competence: A pilot study." *Early Childhood Education Journal* 47, no. 2: 199-206.

Weisz, J.R., A.M. Ugueto, D.M. Cheron, and J. Herren. 2013. "Evidence-based youth psychotherapy in the mental health ecosystem." Journal of *Clinical Child and Adolescent Psychology* 42, no. 2: 274–286.

Wellander, L., M.B. Wells, and I. Feldman. 2016. "Does prevention pay? Costs and potential cost-savings of school interventions targeting children with mental health problems." *The Journal of Mental Health Policy and Economics* 19, no. 2: 91-101.

West, S., R. Puszczynski, and T. Cohn. 2021. "Exploring recreational screen time and social anxiety in adolescents." *Pediatric Nursing* 47, no. 3: 133-140.

Whitney, D. G., and M.D. Peterson. 2019. "US national and state-level prevalence of mental health disorders and disparities of mental health care use in children." *JAMA Pediatrics* 173, no. 4: 389–391.

Wood, J.J., B.D. McLeod, M. Sigman, W.C. Hwang, and B.C. Chu. 2003. "Parenting and childhood anxiety: Theory, empirical findings, and future directions." *Journal of Child Psychology and Psychiatry* 44, no. 1: 134-151.

Wrobel, G. 2020. "Understanding the adoptive family within the context of Christian hospitality." *Dialog: A Journal of Theology* 51, no. 4: 313-322.

Xie, X, Y. Yan, G. Wang, X. Han, and X. Gai. 2018. "The relation between multiple living environment profiles and adolescent self-identity: A person-centered approach." *Child Indicators Research* 12, no. 3: 989-1002.

3. Mental Health and Well-Being in Faith-Based Schools: A Qualitative Study

Beckman, J.E., J.L. Drexler, and K.L. Eames. 2012. "Faithful presence: The Christian school head, personhood, relationships, and outcomes." *Journal of School Choice* 6, no. 1: 104–127.

Collins, S.E., S.L Clifasefi, J. Stanton, K.J.E Straits, E. Gil-Kashiwabara, and P. Rodriguez Espinosa. 2018. "Community-based participatory research (CBPR): Towards equitable involvement of community in psychology research." *The American Psychologist* 73, no. 7: 884–898.

Crouch, A. 2008. *Culture making: Recovering our creative calling.* Downers Grove, IL: InterVarsity Press.

Franbutt, J.M., W. Clark, and G. Speach. 2011. "Supporting mental health and wellness among private school students: A survey of Catholic elementary and secondary schools." *Advances in School Mental Health Promotion* 4, no. 3: 29-41.

Gray, L. M., G. Wong-Wylie, G.R. Rempel, and K. Cook. 2020. "Expanding qualitative research interviewing strategies: Zoom video communications." *The Qualitative Report* 25, no. 5: 1292-1301.

Johnson, E.L. 2010. "A brief history of Christians in psychology." In *Psychology & Christianity: Five Views*, E.L. Johnson (ed.), 9-48. Downers Grove, IL: Inter-Varisty Press.

Maslach, C., W.B. Schaufeli, and M.P. Leiter. 2001. "Job burnout." *Annual Review of Psychology* 52, no. 1: 397-422.

Mikesell, L., E. Bromley, and D. Khodyakov. 2013. "Ethical community-engaged research: A literature review." *American Journal of Public Health* 103, no. 12: 7-14.

Mills, K.A. 2003. "The culture of the Christian school." *Journal of Education & Christian Belief* 7, no. 2: 129–142.

Murray, R.J. 2011. "Hiring school counselors in faith-based schools." *Catholic Education: A Journal of Inquiry & Practice* 15, no. 1: 54–71.

References

Part II: Christian School Perspectives

4. Reflections of a School Counselor

American School Counselor Association (nd). *ASCA National Model*. Available at: https://www.schoolcounselor.org/About-School-Counseling/ASCA-National-Model-for-School-Counseling-Programs.

Rogers, K. 2019. "US teens use screens more than seven hours a day on average—and that's not including school work." CNN, 29 Oct. 2019. Available at: https://www.cnn.com/2019/10/29/health/common-sense-kids-media-use-report-wellness/index.html.

Twenge, J.M., and W.K. Campbell. 2018. "Associations between screen time and lower psychological well-being among children and adolescents: Evidence from a population-based study." *Preventive Medicine Reports* 12:271–283.

5. Trauma-Informed Instruction: A View from the Classroom

Brackett, M. 2019. *Permission to feel: Unlocking the power of emotions to help our kids, ourselves, and our society thrive.* New York: Celadon Books.

Burke Harris, N. 2018. *The deepest well: Healing the long-term effects of childhood adversity.* New York: Houghton Mifflin Harcourt.

Centers for Disease Control. 2021. Adverse Childhood Experiences (ACEs). Available at: https://www.cdc.gov/violenceprevention/aces/index.html.

Costello, B., J. Wachtel, and T. Wachtel. 2019. *The restorative practices handbook: For teachers, disciplinarians and administrators.* Bethlehem, PA: International Institute for Restorative Practices.

Feifer, S. 2019. *The neuro-psychology of stress & trauma: How to develop a trauma informed school.* Middletown, MD: School Neuropsych Press, LLC.

Forbes, H.T. 2012. *Help for Billy: A beyond consequences approach to helping challenging children learn.* Boulder, CO: Beyond Consequences Institute, LLC.

Ginwright, S. 2018. *The future of healing: shifting from trauma informed care to healing centered engagement.* Available at: https://ginwright.medium.com/the-future-of-healing-shifting-from-trauma-informed-care-to-healing-centered-engagement-634f557ce69c.

Grant, S. 2020. *An introduction to creating a trauma informed school in a COVID world.* Available at: https://vimeo.com/ondemand/ticinacovidworld.

Greene, R.W. 2016. *Lost and found: Helping behaviorally challenged students (and, while you're at it, all the others).* San Francisco: Jossey-Bass.

Leeb, R. 2020. "Mental health–related emergency department visits among children aged <18 years during the COVID-19 pandemic — United States, January 1–October 17, 2020." Available at: https://www.cdc.gov/mmwr/volumes/69/wr/mm6945a3.htm.

Perry, B.D., and M. Szalavitz. 2017. *The boy who was raised as a dog: And other stories from a child psychiatrist's notebook.* New York: Basic Books.

Siegel, D., and T. Payne Bryson. 2012. *The whole-brain child: 12 revolutionary strategies to nurture your child's developing mind.* New York: Bantam Books.

Sorrels, B. 2015. *Reaching and teaching children exposed to trauma.* Lewisville, NC: Gryphon House, Inc.

Souers, K., and P. Hall. 2016. *Fostering resilient learners: Strategies for creating a trauma-sensitive classroom.* Alexandria, VA: ASCD.

6. Educator Well-Being: What About Leaders and Teachers?

Land, G. 1998. *Breakthrough and beyond: Mastering the future of today.* Kansas City: Leadership 2000 Inc.

Lee, M.H., R. Djita, and A. Cheng. 2021. "Sabbath practices and wellness in Christian schools." *ACSI Research in Brief* 2, no. 2: 6-10.

Levine, J.A. 2002. "Non-exercise Activity Thermogenesis (NEAT)." *Best Practice & Research: Clinical Endocrinology & Metabolism* 16, no. 4: 679-702.

Mann, A. 2018. "Why we need best friends at work." *Gallup Workplace*, 15 January 2018. Available at: https://www.gallup.com/workplace/236213/why-need-best-friends-work.aspx.

Miller, R., B. Latham, K. Baird, and M. Kinder. 2020. *WHOLE: What teachers need to help students thrive.* San Francisco: Jossey-Bass.

Panchal, N., R. Kamal, C. Cox, and R. Garfield. 2021. "The implications of COVID-19 for mental health and substance use." Kaiser Family Foundation, 10 February 2021. Available at: https://www.kff.org/report-section/the-implications-of-covid-19-for-mental-health-and-substance-use-issue-brief/.

Seligman, M. 2011. *Flourish: A visionary new understanding of happiness and well-being.* New York: Free Press.

Swaner, L.E., and M.H. Lee. 2020. *Christian schools and COVID-19: 2020-2021 school year profile.* Colorado Springs, CO: ACSI.

Swaner, L.E., C.A. Marshall, and S.A. Tesar. 2019. *Flourishing schools: Research on Christian school culture and community.* Colorado Springs, CO: ACSI.

Swoboda, A.J. 2018. *Subversive sabbath: The surprising power of rest in a nonstop world.* Grand Rapids, MI: Brazos Press.

Will, M. 2021. "Teachers are not OK, even though we need them to be." *EdWeek*, 14 September, 2021. Available at: https://www.edweek.org/teaching-learning/teachers-are-not-ok-even-though-we-need-them-to-be/2021/09.

Part III: Programs and Practices

7. Core Components of Student Care

Reeves, M., S. Brock, and K. Cowan. 2008. "Managing school crises: More than just response." *Principal Leadership* 8, no. 9: 10.

Summits Initiative. 2002. *Guidelines for a student support component.* Los Angeles: UCLA.

Available at: http://smhp.psych.ucla.edu/summit2002/guidelinessupportdoc.pdf.

8. Systematizing Support in Christian Schools

Child Mind Institute. 2016. *Children's mental health report.* Available at: https://childmind.org/report/2016-childrens-mental-health-report/.

Dombrowski, E.L., and M.H. Lee. 2020. "The inclusion journey: From program to identity." In L.E. Swaner, ed., *ACSI Leading Insights: Special education and inclusion.* Colorado Springs, CO: Association of Christian Schools International, 70-84.

Haggard, M.S., B. Allen, M. Chamberlain, and M. Flores Bauer. 2007. *School-based mental health needs assessment.* Available at: http://www.allenshea.com/documents/SBMHFinalReport_December2007.pdf.

Vaillancourt, K., K.C. Cowan, and A. Kalamaros Skalski. 2016. "Providing mental health services within a multi-tiered system of supports." *Depression in children and adolescents: Guidelines for school practice.* Bethesda, MD: National Association of School Psychologists.

9. Crisis Intervention in Christian Schools

American Foundation for Suicide Prevention (AFSP), Suicide Prevention Resource Center (SPRC). 2018. *After a suicide: A toolkit for schools,* 2nd ed. Waltham, MA: Education Development Center, Inc.

American School Counselor Association (ASCA). 2021. *School counselor roles and ratios.* Available at: https://www.schoolcounselor.org/About-School-Counseling/School-Counselor-Roles-Ratios.

Curtin, S. 2020. "State suicide rates among adolescents and young adults aged 10–24: United States, 2000–2018." *National Vital Statistics Reports* 69, no. 11. Hyattsville, MD: National Center for Health Statistics.

Joshi, S.V., M. Ojakian, L. Lenoir, and J. Lopez. 2017. *K-12 toolkit for mental health promotion and suicide prevention.* Stanford, CA: HEARD Alliance, Stanford University.

LoMurray, S., D. Adams, J. Anema, and M. Moore. 2021. *Sources of strength trainer manual.* Available at: https://sourcesofstrength.org/wp-content/uploads/TrainerManual_2021B_Print.pdf.

Mueller, A.S., S. Diefendorf, S. Abrutyn, K.A. Beardall, R. Gallagher, J. Jackson, Y. Liang, H. Steinberg, J.T. Watkins, and H. Worton. 2021. "Strategies to improve youth suicide prevention in schools & communities." Social Worlds & Youth Well-Being Research Paper. Bloomington, IN: Indiana University Bloomington.

National Action Alliance for Suicide Prevention Clinical Care & Intervention Task Force. 2012. *Suicide care in systems framework.* Available at: http://actionallianceforsuicideprevention.org/sites/actionallianceforsuicideprevention.org/files/taskforces/.

Stone, C. 2021. "Suicide assessments: American School Counselor Association

(ASCA): The medical profession affirms the school counselor's truth." *American School Counselor Association Magazine*, July-August, 2021.

Suicide Prevention Resource Center (SPRC). 2014. "Suicide screening and assessment." Available at: https://www.sprc.org/sites/default/files/migrate/library/RS_suicide%20screening_91814%20final.pdf.

U.S. Department of Health & Human Services. 2021. "U.S. Surgeon General issues advisory on youth mental health crisis further exposed by COVID-19 pandemic." Available at: https://www.hhs.gov/about/news/2021/12/07/us-surgeon-general-issues-advisory-on-youth-mental-health-crisis-further-exposed-by-covid-19-pandemic.html.

ABOUT THE AUTHORS

Cara Dixon, LPC, NCC is the chief executive officer of Growth Minded Counseling and Consulting and a seminar leader at the University of Pennsylvania. Prior to these roles, Cara was the founder and lead accreditation officer of a partial hospitalization program, and the director of counseling services at a Christian boarding and day school. Cara has supervised teams in both clinical and school-based settings for years to provide high quality mental health support services to individuals. She has written blogs, been interviewed for podcasts, and given seminars on the topic of mental health in Christian schools.

Nancy Gillespie is a licensed school counselor and has served at Grove City Christian School (GCCS) outside of Columbus, Ohio, for the past thirteen years. At GCCS, she has created a comprehensive school counseling program and continues to manage students' needs in the areas of academic success, personal social development, and college and career options. Concurrently, she is a first-year doctoral student in pursuit of her Ph.D. in counselor education and supervision from The Ohio State University. Working at a Christian school gives her the opportunity to share her love of education, counseling, and people with the love of Christ at the center.

Kelsey Hauser is research assistant for the School Counselor Mental Health Initiative and a master's level graduate student in clinical counseling and school counseling at Denver Seminary. She has a background in education as a licensed substitute teacher and special education paraprofessional.

Ginger Hill is the founder of Good Health for Good Works, where she helps the earnest, but often exhausted, workers in Christian organizations take steps toward healthier living so they can stay well to serve well and effectively fulfill their God-given calling. She supports Christian organizations through employee wellness seminars, coaching, and consulting. As an ACSI Ministry Partner, Ginger has a special place in her heart for teachers. In her career, she has worked with individual teachers to help them develop strategies for healthy living within their demanding profession and presented wellness seminars to Chicago public school teachers as part of the Chicago Lives Healthy program. Ginger has over twenty years of experience in the employee wellness industry and is a committed Christian who seeks to apply biblical principles to every area of life, including helping people to improve their health.

Charlotte Marshall Powell is fueled by opportunities to connect people with research that makes a lasting impact. Knowing the usefulness of data in developing innovative solutions, Dr. Marshall Powell joined Barna in July 2021 as vice president of research. Prior to joining Barna, she served as a senior researcher at ACSI, and also served previously as a tenure track psychology professor and taught undergraduate and graduate psychology courses. She holds a B.A in psychology from Spelman College and a Ph.D. in psychology from the University of Delaware.

Elizabeth Meier Thornton is an adjunct professor at Denver Seminary in the school and clinical counseling programs and is an adjunct professor at Denver University in the school counseling program. She works full-time as a middle school counselor at Peak to Peak Charter School, and has been a school counselor in public, private, and charter schools in the United States and globally, including one ACSI school. She is a licensed school counselor and licensed professional counselor in the state of Colorado and is a national certified counselor. A 2012 Denver Seminary graduate from the master's in clinical and school counseling Program, she has worked with the School Counseling Mental Health Initiative (SCMHI) as a research associate, and is currently working toward a Ph.D. in counselor education and supervision from the University of the Cumberlands.

Brittany Miller is a research associate with the School Counseling Mental Health Initiative (SCMHI) at Denver Seminary. As part of the SCMHI team, Brittany has the opportunity to partner with public, private, and charter schools to research student mental health. She graduated with honors from Denver Seminary with her dual concentration Master of Arts in clinical mental health and school counseling, and she is a Licensed Professional Counselor and a National Certified Counselor. Her work focuses on the biopsychosocial and faith aspects of child and young adult development and the various school and treatment systems they encounter throughout their lives.

Laura Miller is a certified Colorado music educator and passionate teacher who has taught a variety of subjects nationally and internationally in Oklahoma, Colorado, Thailand, and Jordan. Laura is now pursuing her masters with a dual concentration in clinical mental health and school counseling at Denver Seminary.

Rex Miller launched MindShift, a faith-based research and coaching organization, in 2013. He is the author of *Humanizing the Education Machine* and *WHOLE: What Teachers Need to Help Students Thrive,* as well as the facilitator for the Christian education *MindShift.* Rex's current vision is to help every student embrace and hold on to their God-given genius and help adults rediscover theirs. He recently released *The Genius Spark* and a free app to support this vision. Rex has received the CoreNet Global Innovator of the Year award, CoreNet's Industry Excellent Award, IFMA's Luminary Author's award, and was named a Texas A&M Professional Fellow. He serves clients such as Google, Microsoft, Facebook, Disney, Amazon, GoDaddy, and the U.S. federal government. Rex recently moved to Glen Rose, Texas, and purchased River Rose, a ranch and leadership center.

Brooke Volpone is pursuing her Masters of Arts degree in counseling, with a school counseling concentration. Brooke has worked with adolescents for much of her adult life and looks forward to continuing to empower and advocate for students as a school counselor, post-graduation.

Jon Widmier is an adjunct professor at Denver Seminary in the school counseling program. He also serves as the coordinator of social-emotional and behavioral services for Littleton Public Schools in Littleton, Colorado. A school counselor by trade, he has served districts by helping to develop danger assessment protocols and as a member of their crisis teams, as well as 504 management, individual career and academic plans, social-emotional learning, multitiered systems of support, and safety team leadership.

Dr. Adam Wilson is the chair of the school counseling program at Denver Seminary and the director of the School Counseling Mental Health Initiative (SCMHI), a research initiative seeking to better understand effective mental health interventions in schools. He is also a licensed professional counselor, working predominantly with children, adolescents, and their families. His clinical work focuses on areas such as anxiety, ADHD, and depression. Adam is the co-author of the chapter "The Neurobiology of Stress and Trauma" in the book *Treating Trauma in Christian Counseling*, edited by H. D. Gingrich and F. C. Gingrich (2017). Adam is a Colorado native and enjoys the outdoors, where he and his family love to play.

Betsy Winkle is a school psychologist who combines her passion for education and reconciliation in her role as director of education services at All Belong: A Center for Inclusive Education. Fueled by a desire to help each child flourish and develop their God-given gifts, Betsy enjoys walking alongside parents and teachers to help them understand how each struggling child thinks and learns, and creating structures within schools that support all students. She is particularly interested in the impact of life circumstances and mental health on a child's educational success. Betsy received her Bachelor of Arts in psychology from Calvin College and her Master of Arts and educational specialist degrees in school psychology from Lehigh University.

About the Series Editor

Dr. Lynn E. Swaner is the chief strategy and innovation officer at ACSI, where she leads initiatives and develops strategies to address compelling questions and challenges facing Christian education. Dr. Swaner serves as a Cardus Senior Fellow and is a Licensed Mental Health Counselor (LMHC). She is the co-author or editor of multiple books on Christian education, including *Flourishing Together: A Christian Vision for Students, Educators, and Schools* and *MindShift: Catalyzing Change in Christian Education*. Prior to joining ACSI, she served as a professor of education and a Christian school administrator in New York.

ACSI
STRONGER TOGETHER

It's Time To Flourish

Think for a moment: In 100 years, what legacy do you want to leave for the students who sat in your classrooms? ACSI wants to come alongside you and help your school community flourish how God intends—biblically.

ACSI has been leading Christ-centered education toward excellence for more than 40 years, always seeking to understand what truly impacts and improves a Christian school. Through a multiyear endeavor, ACSI Research identified thirty-five constructs that support five primary domains of flourishing, which contribute to a school community marked by healthy spiritual, emotional, and cultural characteristics. This research was validated by a rigorous independent review and has blossomed into the ACSI Flourishing Initiative, which aligns ACSI Research, Professional Development, and Accreditation with a focus on flourishing students, educators, and Christian schools.

ACSI *Leading Insights: Special Education* advances Christ-centered education by focusing on schools' responsiveness to special needs, which is a validated construct in the flourishing domain of Expertise & Resources.

To learn more, please visit acsi.org/flourishing.